Christmas Drama for Youth

Sarah Walton Miller

BROADMAN PRESS
Nashville, Tennessee

4275-11
ISBN: 0-8054-7511-7

Dewey Decimal Classification: 812
Subject heading: CHRISTMAS PLAYS

Library of Congress Catalog Card Number: 76-20255
Printed in the United States of America

Contents

Foreword

Are you looking for something dramatic for Christmas? Somewhere in the variety in this book may be just what you want. The settings are divided between biblical and contemporary. There are two one-act plays and a carol worship service, each requiring about thirty-five minutes to play. There are short things, such as skits, choral readings, and monologues. There is an entire dramatic party with four fun drama skits included as well as a Christmas game.

All are simple to stage, even in the most limited situations. There are parts for those as young as eight and as old as eighty. It's more fun to cast by age and more believable. If the innkeeper is supposed to be fifty, a man of fifty will play the part better than a young teenager. Youth and age mix well in drama and have a wonderful time.

1
The Dowry

Cast

Jephthah, innkeeper at Bethlehem, about 50 years old
Leah, his wife, about the same age
Esther, their housekeeper, widow of Jephthah's brother Joel, about 30
Merab, her daughter, 15
Obed, 16, indentured stableboy and servant
Isaac, an old beggar who does his begging at the inn
Joash, a young shepherd, 17
Elam, his father, also a shepherd

Scene

The yard behind the inn. The stable is off right, the inn off left. Realism is unnecessary. Place a plain rough bench at either side of the stage, a third bench against a "well" in center stage. Make the well of cardboard painted to resemble stone, 2 to 2½ feet high.

Props: A water jar or ewer, a plain blanket, crude crutch for Isaac.

Time: As the play begins, after sundown. As it ends, after midnight.

Costumes

For costume ideas, see pictures from Sunday School literature. All women wear long tunics with long sleeves and high necks. All have hair covered with a short scarf. Around their waists are girdles or sashes. All wear sandals, as do the men, except Isaac. Merab and Esther wear small aprons, their tunics old and drab. Dyed old sheets are excellent for these. Leah's tunic is of better color and appearance. She wears metal bracelets and coins on a band around her forehead. She may wear a short surcoat, similar to today's sleeveless jackets, which can be removed for the last scene.

The men wear tunics also. Jephthah's is a better color and has wide bands of contrasting color at hem and sleeves. It is long. He wears a wide contrasting girdle wrapped around like a cummerbund and a long surcoat. His turban has coins on the front, and he wears a gold chain around his neck.

The two shepherds wear plain faded tunics, heavy plain surcoats (possibly from bedspreads or draperies) with long sleeves. Their headdresses are typical of the biblical shepherd with a band around the head and extra length to protect from the weather.

Obed wears a short faded tunic with short sleeves, a narrow girdle, and no headdress (if his hair is short, cover with a small turban).

Old Isaac wears a ragged, faded tunic; a ragged, faded large surcoat; a ragged headdress similar to the shepherds but shorter; and his feet are bound in rags. His crutch is beside him.

Note: In Bible times girls married at age thirteen and fourteen.

(*As the play begins, old Isaac the beggar is sitting on the bench by the inn. Jephthah and Leah enter right, from the stable. Obed trails behind them.*)

LEAH (*angry*): I still say it's a mistake to take them in! Go back and tell them you've changed your mind!

JEPHTHAH: I can't do that. Besides it's only the stable.

LEAH: The stable is still part of the inn! That girl is about to have a baby. Jephthah, don't expect me to be a midwife!

JEPHTHAH (*appeasing*): No, indeed. My love, consider: it's only for one day. Don't forget they paid as much as for a room in the inn.

LEAH (*angry*): I don't care! Money isn't everything. You should have sent them away!

JEPHTHAH (*growing angry*): It's easy for you to talk! Who spends money for goods from the Greek peddlers? Not me, that's sure! It's one thing to buy a length of blue for a sabbath tunic when all the other wives weave and dye their own cloth. It's another to figure out a way to pay for it!

LEAH (*complaining*): You begrudge me a tunic after all I do to keep this business going?

JEPHTHAH (*angry*): I don't begrudge you anything! I indulge you, woman!

LEAH: Why didn't you indulge me by sending those Nazarenes on their way? If she decides to have that baby in the night, don't waken me!

(*She flounces left into the inn. Jephthah glares after her then shouts at Obed.*)

JEPHTHAH: Boy! Get busy! Those people are staying! Go stable their donkey.

OBED (*grinning*): I did, sir.

JEPHTHAH: When?

OBED: When they were inside talking to you.

JEPHTHAH: Well, Mr. Know-it-all, why did you stable him before I agreed they could stay?

OBED (*boldly*): Oh, sir, I couldn't see you letting money get away.

JEPHTHAH (*angrily*): Some day I'm going to kick you out of here!

OBED (*unruffled*): Not before my six years are up.

JEPHTHAH: Go look after the animals of my guests!

OBED: I did.

JEPHTHAH: You fed and watered them all?

OBED: Yes.

JEPHTHAH (*frustrated*): Well, go do something! Go help that couple get settled! I don't like to see you idle!

OBED: Yes, sir. (*He disappears into stable, right.*)

JEPHTHAH (*pausing by Isaac*): You're another parasite! Just because you choose to beg outside my inn, don't expect any favors from me!

ISAAC (*humbly*): No, master.

JEPHTHAH: Don't bother my guests, either!

ISAAC: No, master.

JEPHTHAH (*grumbling*): At least you came back here where no one can see you.

ISAAC: It's warmer here. Besides the inn is full. More guests are unlikely.

JEPHTHAH: Some still try. The Romans did a good turn for Bethlehem ordering this census. The town is full. Many will sleep in the fields this night. Consider yourself fortunate to have this bench! But stay back here!

ISAAC: Oh, yes, master.

(*Jephthah leaves left. Then Joash enters left stealthily. Sees Isaac, puts his finger to his lips, crosses to the right. Isaac raises his hand, then pretends to doze. Merab enters from left with empty water jar. She runs to meet Joash, leaving ewer by the well. She would not have greeted him by an embrace or a kiss, but by giving him her hands.*)

MERAB: Joash!

JOASH (*taking her hands*): Merab! I waited by the olive grove, but you didn't come!

MERAB: We have been so busy. The inn is full with all those coming to register. Aunt Leah would have noticed my absence.

JOASH: Have you a moment now?

MERAB: Perhaps. The guests are all fed and soon will bed down for the night, I hope.

JOASH: Good!

MERAB: Joash, you must go. If my uncle finds you here, who knows what he will do?

JOASH (*rashly*): I'm not afraid of him.

MERAB: I am! He will find a way to punish my mother and me.

JOASH: Oh, Merab, I don't want that! But I must see you. Why does the world seem determined to keep apart those who should be together?

MERAB: If only my father were alive. If only I had a dowry! Then your father would welcome me as a daughter-in-law.

JOASH: Father likes you, Merab. It's not that. He says the dowry is a custom that assures independence for a new marriage. If he were rich. . . . Oh, Merab, I'd gladly be poor with you!

MERAB (*tenderly*): Oh, Joash.

JOASH: The dowry means nothing to me. My love, you are my Merab, whose price is far above rubies!

MERAB (*hopefully*): Maybe my uncle . . .? (*She pulls away and sits glumly on the well bench.*) No, he won't!

JOASH (*sits beside her*): Your uncle give you a dowry? That's a foolish dream. Not as long as he has you and Esther for unpaid servants.

MERAB: But, Joash, he did take us in when Father died.

JOASH: He had to. It's the law. No, don't expect help from your uncle. We must find another way.

(*Obed enters from stable. Quietly listens. Old Isaac is still dozing on his bench.*)

MERAB (*glumly*): What way?

JOASH: I don't know. But things must change. Who knows what can happen? Why, soon we will be adding another shepherd.

MERAB: Another?

JOASH: Yes. The flock has grown so, my father and brother and I need help. If the flock continues to grow, perhaps my father will relent. Then we could marry without the dowry.

MERAB: If only he would.

JOASH (*teasing, trying to cheer her*): I will dangle temptation before his eyes. A daughter-in-law who weaves, who tends animals, who cooks! Four shepherds would fare well under her care!

MERAB: Oh, Joash, is it only a dream?

JOASH: I must dream! (*He holds her hand lovingly against his cheek, then rises.*) I must go, my love. The lost sheep I went to find are still lost. Tomorrow?

MERAB: Yes. By the grove.

(*He leaves left. Merab picks up the ewer to dip into the well. Obed comes to her.*)

OBED (*smiling*): So Joash was here.

MERAB (*nervously*): You saw him?

OBED: And heard. (*At her involuntary gesture of fear*) Oh, don't worry. I won't tell. Merab, you are wasting your time. You never will be able to marry Joash.

MERAB: Don't say that! Obed, I love him so much.

OBED (*sits on well bench, speaks flippantly*): What is love? It is many things. There are many kinds of love. Even the love I have for you.

MERAB: Don't tease! Obed, you are my friend. But that is all.

OBED: Well, in one more year, I will have paid my father's debt to Jephthah. The six year's servitude will be up. Then I will be a free man.

MERAB (*in sympathy*): I am sorry for you, Obed. Being an orphan must be—at least I have my mother.

OBED (*lightly*): Oh, I don't mind it now. I used to resent my father's dying and leaving me with his debt. A boy of eleven thinks of six years as eternity. But five have gone and only one to go.

MERAB: I'm glad.

OBED: I don't even resent my father any more.

MERAB: That's good.

OBED: Merab, listen! (*He looks around to detect any eavesdroppers. Old Isaac appears to be sleeping.*) If I tell you something will you keep it to yourself?

MERAB: Of course.

OBED: Well, when I go out of here a free man, I won't be a pauper. Jephthah has no idea!

MERAB: What do you mean?

OBED: All these years, as I tended their animals and fetched and carried for them, guests of this inn have rewarded me. Sometimes little, sometimes generously. It's quite a sum now. You'd be surprised. So would Jephthah.

MERAB: Why don't you pay off the debt?

OBED: And go out penniless? Now you are the only one who knows this. Keep it secret.

MERAB: I won't tell. What will you do with the money?

OBED (*with an air of importance*): Start a business. Just a small one at first. Maybe a herd of donkeys to carry wares from place to place. Wherever the merchants want.

MERAB (*approvingly*): That's a good business. You are smart, Obed. You will do well. I know it.

OBED: Merab, do you ever think—by next year you will be past marriageable age?

MERAB: I know.

OBED: Maybe then you'll know you'll never marry Joash. Unless you take him when you are both *really* old. Maybe you'll change your mind about me.

MERAB (*gently*): No, Obed.

OBED (*generously*): I'm not hard to please. I don't mind if you'll be sixteen! I'll take you without a dowry, too.

MERAB: No, Obed.

OBED: What do I want with your dowry? One day I'll be a rich man on my own. You could be rich, too.

MERAB: For your sake, I hope all things work out well. But Obed, I won't change my mind.

OBED (*cheerfully*): I'll wait. A lot of things can change in a year.

MERAB (*laughs*): You are hopeless! I must go. Leah said to take water to the guests in the stable. Are there really guests in the stable?

OBED: Just peasants. Galileans. A man and his wife from Nazareth. A carpenter, he says.

MERAB: But—the stable?

OBED (*with pride*): It's clean. They couldn't find any place to stay. Besides his wife is about to have a baby and is tired.

MERAB: A baby? They've come all the way from Nazareth and she is—? It doesn't make sense. He could register without her. Why did she travel at such a time?

OBED (*shrugs*): Who knows? Love, maybe. Go on. Take the water.

(*Merab dips ewer in well and lifts it out, apparently full. Places it on her shoulder and leaves right. Obed walks over and sits by Isaac.*)

OBED: Don't try to fool me, old one. You aren't asleep. I know you were listening.

ISAAC: Eh? What did you say?

OBED: You old fox. You heard all right. You know everything that goes on around here.

ISAAC: Maybe.

OBED: Maybe nothing: I'm surprised Jephthah lets you beg around the inn at all.

ISAAC (*humorously*): What other place in Bethlehem has its very own beggar? Besides, how would it look if he drove away an old crippled beggar who doesn't do anyone any harm?

Jephthah is a great one for wanting things to look right to the town. He places great importance on what people think. Me? I stay because it's the best place to beg. Strangers coming in every day.

(*Esther enters from left.*)

ESTHER: Good-evening, Obed. Isaac.

OBED: Good-evening, Esther.

ISAAC: Esther.

ESTHER: Obed, have you seen Merab?

OBED: She's in the stable.

ESTHER: Stable?

OBED: Leah told her to take water to the couple there.

ESTHER (*surprised*): Two people are staying in the stable?

OBED: And likely to be three before morning, I'd guess.

ESTHER: Oh, dear, is that right? Then I'd better go see for myself. (*Leaves right.*)

ISAAC: There goes a good woman. Too bad her husband died leaving her nothing. Oh, well, Jephthah has his faults; but he did provide for his brother's wife and daughter.

OBED (*laughs in derision*): Oh, he's good, he is!

ISAAC (*puzzled*): That's what I said.

OBED (*scoffing*): Like nothing! I know a secret, old man!

(*They are interrupted by Elam's entrance left.*)

ELAM (*loudly*): Obed, have you seen Joash?

OBED (*calmly*): Is he lost?

ELAM: He's going to wish he were if he's here!

OBED: You don't see him, do you?

(*Jephthah enters from left.*)

JEPHTHAH (*annoyed*): Here! What's going on? Oh, it's you, Elam.

ELAM: I said, "Is Joash here?"

JEPHTHAH: He'd better not be! Now look here, Elam. You keep that boy away from Merab!

ELAM: Where is that girl?

OBED: She's in the stable with Esther.

ELAM (*going right and calling*): Merab! Merab!

(*Merab enters with ewer.*)

MERAB: Oh! I—I thought I heard my name.

ELAM: You did. Is Joash here?

MERAB (*nervously*): N—no.

ELAM: Has he been here?

OBED (*quickly*): Lots of times! You know that, Elam. Where's he supposed to be now?

ELAM: Out hunting strayed sheep.

JEPHTHAH: Then maybe that's where he is.

ELAM: The sheep came in by themselves.

MERAB: Maybe he doesn't know that. Maybe he's still hunting for them.

ELAM: All right. I'll look again.

JEPHTHAH (*angrily*): Elam, you keep that boy away from this inn. You hear me?

ELAM: Jephthah, does it ever bother you, we old men keep those two young people apart?

JEPHTHAH: Certainly not!

ELAM: There's nothing I can do but keep them apart for their own good. But you are a wealthy man.

JEPHTHAH: Gossip! Only gossip! I barely make ends meet.

ELAM: We know better than that. You could give that girl a dowry and never miss it.

JEPHTHAH: Impossible! No one understands my expenses.

ELAM: Any time you do, they have my blessing. Until you do, I am as anxious to keep him away from here as you are. For both their sakes.

(*Elam leaves left. Esther enters right.*)

ESTHER: Merab, come! I need you. (*The two leave right.*)

JEPHTHAH: What's going on?

OBED: I don't know for sure, but I expect that young woman is soon to give birth. The one in the stable.

JEPHTHAH (*angrily*): I won't have it!

ISAAC (*humorously*): What can you do about it?

JEPHTHAH (*shakes fist at old man*): One more word out of you, old man, and out you go! Do you hear? Now, Obed, go get Esther and Merab at once.

(*Obed goes to stable and returns with Esther and Merab.*)

JEPHTHAH: All right! Now what's going on?

ESTHER: The girl Mary is in labor.

JEPHTHAH (*loudly*): That's all I need! Are you trying to put me out of business?

(*Leah enters.*)

LEAH: Jephthah, why are you yelling? You can be heard all over the inn!

OBED (*enjoying the to-do*): The peasant couple in the stable are about to become parents.

JEPHTHAH: How can they do this to me? Wasn't I kind and let them have shelter in my stable when there was no other place for them?

LEAH (*spitefully*): For regular pay, don't forget! See where your greed has got you? I told you this would happen. I say it again, don't you count on me, Jephthah! I refuse to help that woman. There's work to do with our guests! I'm busy!

ESTHER: I could help her, Jephthah.

JEPHTHAH: If you are out here sitting around the stable, who will do your work? Esther, it costs me money to provide for you and Merab.

ESTHER (*gratefully*): Thank you, Jephthah. I am grateful.

JEPHTHAH: I should hope so. But I'm not a rich man, You and Merab must help.

OBED (*boldly*): They do the work of four servants!

JEPHTHAH: Who asked you?

OBED: You know if they left you'd have to pay four servants to take their places.

JEPHTHAH: Nonsense! Why should they leave? Where else would a widow and orphan find so good a home?

ESTHER: Jephthah, let me help this young woman. It seems the best answer to the problem. Merab and Obed can take my place inside. Will you do this, Obed?

OBED: Sure. Come on, Merab. That is, if our kind mistress is willing!

LEAH: (*disagreeably*): Oh, all right. Come on. Just don't you call on me, Esther!

(*Leah, Merab and Obed go left.*)

JEPHTHAH: I suppose this is best. All right, stay with them, Esther. Get it over quickly.

ISAAC: I doubt if Esther has much say in the matter.

JEPHTHAH: Hold your tongue, old man!

(*Jephthah leaves left.*)

ESTHER: It will be a while yet. Babies usually aren't in a hurry. I will get water ready.

(*She gets ewer and dips water from the well. Places ewer on bench.*)

ISAAC: Is it well with the young mother?

ESTHER: She's a strong, healthy girl.

ISAAC: That is good.

ESTHER: She's just the age of my Merab. She has a sweetness about her, Isaac. There's something special—I don't know.

ISAAC: I trust the father-to-be is holding up well?

ESTHER (*laughs*): He is nervous for his young wife. He is a good man. There is an earthy wisdom.

ISAAC: Then the child should be healthy and happy. Once I had a son.

ESTHER (*as she sits by him*): I didn't know that.

ISAAC: Oh it is long ago. My wife was a plain cheerful woman. She bore this beautiful boy child. I was a seller of purple in those days.

ESTHER: Imagine.

ISAAC: One day I decided to travel to Egypt to purchase supplies. Rebecca teased and teased to go along and take Ephraim. I said no, but finally gave in. We joined a large caravan. Out in the desert, marauders attacked. We were overpowered. Rebecca and Ephraim were killed, and I was left for dead in the desert. Some friendly nomads found me and cared for me. They saved my life; but I was left as you see, a cripple. I lost my family, my business, and my good legs.

ESTHER: Isaac, I didn't know. How I grieve for you.

ISAAC: Oh, it is long ago now. In some ways life has been good. I have met good people and bad. You are one of the good ones, Esther.

ESTHER (*rising*): You embarrass me. I must go see about my charge.

ISAAC: What is her name?

ESTHER: Mary. Her husband is Joseph. Take your rest now, Isaac.

(She leaves right. He sits alone briefly. Then Obed enters from the left.)

OBED: Still awake? (*He sits by Isaac.*)

ISAAC: Esther has kept me company. I was remembering. You did what was needed?

OBED: Merab is finishing up. Then everyone will be settled. As much as an inn full of people can be settled.

ISAAC: She is a good girl. She really loves Joash, you know.

OBED: She is young. She'll get over it. You'll see. Then maybe. . . .

ISAAC: Don't count on it. You waste your time.

OBED: It's my time.

ISAAC: Obed, you can make something of your life if you will.

OBED: I know. And I will.

ISAAC: Once I had a son. He'd be about your age now. I couldn't watch him grow up, but I have watched you these five years. Your own father. . . .

OBED (*sharply*): Let's not talk about him.

ISAAC: He didn't do this to you on purpose.

OBED (*harshly*): He was a fool to get into debt to Jephthah!

ISAAC: You don't know the circumstances. Had he lived. . . .

OBED: But he didn't. And Jephthah is not a man to overlook a debt. Someday Jephthah is due for a shock!

ISAAC: Your secret? You mentioned a secret.

OBED: Can I trust you not to tell?

ISAAC: I survive by being neutral and keeping secrets.

OBED: I bet you do!

ISAAC: Don't tell me if you don't trust me after all this time.

OBED (*looks to see no one is listening*): Well, once, oh, a long time back, I overheard Leah and Jephthah quarreling about some money. He wanted to use the money to add on to the inn. She called him reckless and a fool to spend what wasn't his. They kept on quarreling, and then I understood. This was money his brother had left to care for Esther and for Merab's dowry.

ISAAC (*astonished*): Merab's dowry? But Merab has no dowry!

OBED (*knowingly*): Oh, yes she has! But she doesn't know about it.

ISAAC: Oh, Obed, why didn't you tell her?

OBED: I forgot all about what I heard. It was so long ago. Lately I've been remembering. All this talk about a dowry brought it back.

ISAAC: Obed, why haven't you told Merab and Esther about this money?

OBED: And lose her to Joash? You think I'm without my senses?

ISAAC: How can you keep this secret knowing her unhappiness?

OBED: She'll get over it.

ISAAC (*sadly*): My boy, you are piling up misery for yourself.

OBED: No! I'm protecting myself!

ISAAC: Will you be happy with Merab's unhappiness?

OBED: One day I'll be rich. Merab will have everything she wants.

ISAAC: You think that will make her happy? Then you don't know Merab.

OBED (*rises, threatening*): You are too old to understand! Remember, not a word of this if you value your miserable life!

ISAAC: I won't tell her. But you must.

OBED (*jeers*): Do you think I am daft?

ISAAC: I think you misjudge yourself. You will tell her.

OBED: Go to sleep, old man!

(*Obed goes to bench by stable. Merab enters from left with a blanket over her arm.*)

MERAB: Isaac? Are you still awake?

ISAAC: Yes.

MERAB: I thought Mother might need this coverlet. It grows cold in the night.

ISAAC: Perhaps she will. You are a good girl, Merab.

MERAB (*pleased*): That is a compliment! Thank you, Isaac.

(*She crosses to right.*)

OBED: All finished inside?

MERAB: Yes. For the time at least.

(*She goes off right.*)

ISAAC: Can you hear me, Obed?

OBED (*doesn't answer for a moment, then sullenly*): What do you want now, old man?

ISAAC: You are a smart boy, Obed, but at the same time you are a fool.

OBED (*irritated*): What kind of saying is that?

ISAAC: It isn't a saying. It's the truth.

OBED (*harshly*): Go to sleep!

(*Jephthah enters left.*)

JEPHTHAH: Any news?

ISAAC: No, master.

JEPHTHAH (*fretting*): Why is she taking so long?

ISAAC: Babies are their own timekeepers. (*He pulls his cloak over him and lays on the bench to sleep.*)

(*Jephthah goes toward stable and turns back to the well. He is standing thinking when Leah enters left.*)

LEAH: Here you are. Why don't you come to bed?

JEPHTHAH: In a minute.

LEAH: Why are you standing there?

JEPHTHAH: Nothing. No reason.

LEAH: Then come on. Morning will be here soon enough.

JEPHTHAH (*crossly*): Go to bed, woman! I'll be there soon. Go on!

(*Leah flounces out. Jephthah walks restlessly across to stable, looks in and then returns to well. Obed follows him, speaks softly.*)

OBED: May I speak with you?

JEPHTHAH (*crossly*): I'm going to bed. Another time.

OBED (*casually*): Very well. I can go tell the elders, I guess.

JEPHTHAH (*alerted*): Tell the elders? Tell them what?

OBED: When one has information that affects the fortune and well being of someone else, he should tell the elders. Then they can see the wrong made right.

JEPHTHAH: What wrong? What are you talking about?

OBED: Only the wrong to Merab and Esther!

JEPHTHAH (*alarmed, grabs Obed by the shoulders and shakes him hard*): What are you saying? What do you know?

OBED (*angry*): Turn me loose! I know everything.

JEPHTHAH: Everything?

OBED: Everything. The money. Merab's dowry.

JEPHTHAH (*blustering*): Lies! There is no money! Merab has no dowry!

OBED: It's no use. I heard you and your wife talking about it long ago. About your brother, Joel, leaving money for Esther and for Merab's dowry. If the elders look into the matter, they can easily find proof.

(Jephthah sinks to bench, dismayed. Obed watches him, then sits beside him.)

OBED (*slyly*): No one need ever know.

JEPHTHAH: What do you mean? What are you up to?

OBED: I mean there is a way. If you take it, you won't have to go before the elders. Think of the disgrace of being branded a thief.

JEPHTHAH: I am not a thief! I have not touched that money!

OBED: Thanks to Leah. I heard that, too. She's a better wife than you deserve. At least she kept you from using it. But who will believe that?

JEPHTHAH (*weakly*): See here! How dare you talk like that to me? I—I can have you whipped.

OBED: But you won't. I wouldn't advise it. Listen to me. There is a way to save yourself. And you can *keep* the money! No one can say I'm not generous.

JEPHTHAH (*after a pause*): I'm listening.

OBED: Jephthah, in one year I'll be a free man.

JEPHTHAH: You keep reminding me.

OBED: On the day I'm free, give me Merab for my wife. I will take her without a dowry.

JEPHTHAH: You want Merab that much?

OBED: Yes! As her guardian you can give consent to this marriage. Actually you can force her to agree.

JEPHTHAH: The silly girl loves Joash. How will you cope with that?

OBED: Don't worry about that. Not that you would of course. Just say yes and the thing is settled. You will be free and so will I.

JEPHTHAH (*curious*): You trust me?

OBED: Of course. Besides, I could always go to the elders and be revenged. What do you say?

JEPHTHAH: Why have you kept silent all this time?

OBED: At first because it meant nothing to me. Then because it suited me. I look out after my own interests.

JEPHTHAH: I believe you. Why don't you demand your freedom now?

OBED: And have everyone wonder what I have on you? Oh, no. I'll serve out my year. Well, what do you say? Merab for my silence?

JEPHTHAH: Very well. It's a bargain.

OBED (*kindly, as he stands*): Now you'd better go rest. You've had a hard day.

JEPHTHAH: I think so! Obed you are—well no matter.

(*Jephthah leaves left. Obed returns to bench by stable.*)

ISAAC: Obed?

OBED: I hear you.

ISAAC: So did I—hear you, I mean.

OBED: So?

ISAAC: You can't do this.

OBED: Watch me!

ISAAC: You really care about Merab, you know.

OBED: Then don't you say one word to spoil my chances, old man! Or you'll regret it! I mean that! Do you hear?

ISAAC: I hear. But you'll see. Wait. You'll see.

(*Esther enters right.*)

ESTHER: Oh, you are awake, Obed. He's here! A fine boy child.

ISAAC: The young mother?

ESTHER: Isaac awake too? Oh, Mary is fine. A bit weary but happy.

ISAAC: The father survives I take it?

ESTHER (*laughs*): Oh, yes!

(*Merab joins her mother. With Obed they walk to well.*)

MERAB: Oh, Isaac, you should see him! He's beautiful!

ISAAC: It's been my observation that all newborn babies look very much like newborn puppies. Maybe redder and more wrinkled.

ESTHER (*laughs*): Isaac, you are scandalous. This is a beautiful baby.

MERAB: He isn't red and wrinkled. He looks right at you.

ISAAC (*scoffing*): He can't see you. Not really.

MERAB: Yes, he can! I don't care what other babies do! He *sees* you! Obed, come see!

OBED: Oh, no!

MERAB: Yes, you must! Prove to Isaac this is an unusual baby. (*She takes his hand and pulls him to the stable.*) Come on, Obed! You must come!

ISAAC: Better go, Obed. One day you will be a father and this will be your chance to see the result.

ESTHER: Isaac, you really are scandalous! Go on, Obed. It's all right.

(*Merab and Obed leave right. Esther sits on well bench.*)

ISAAC: Tired?

ESTHER: Not really. Just content. This has been a good night. Isaac, there *is* something special about this baby.

ISAAC: Special?

ESTHER: It's hard to describe.

ISAAC: He has feet and hands and all the equipment of the usual baby, doesn't he?

ESTHER: Oh, he's a real baby. A healthy, beautiful boy. No, it's something else. He's just not like other babies. The parents too—they're different.

ISAAC: They are just plain people, aren't they?

ESTHER: Of course. But it's more. A sort of *quality*, if you know what I mean.

ISAAC: Afraid I don't. To me, babies are babies.

(*Merab returns and sits by her mother.*)

ESTHER: Where is Obed?

MERAB: He's moving some hay over to make a more comfortable bed for Mary and Joseph. Mother, what is it about this baby? Or don't you feel it?

ESTHER: Yes, I feel it. I don't know.

MERAB: Obed felt it, too. When we went in, Obed just stood there and looked at him for the longest time. He didn't answer Mary when she spoke to him. He just kept looking at that baby. I really believed the baby knew it, too! Finally, I said we must go. He didn't answer me. Just started moving hay!

(*Joash and Elam enter, excited and breathless. Merab rises.*)

ELAM: Where is he?

ESTHER: Who?

JOASH (*panting*): We've come to see him!

ESTHER: What are you talking about?

ELAM (*excited*): The newborn baby wrapped in swaddling clothes and lying in a manger! He's here, isn't he?

MERAB (*bewildered*): Yes, but he's just born so how could you know?

JOASH: I knew it! The voices were real!

ISAAC: Real?

JOASH: The voices that told us to come here to find a baby, just as Father said, wrapped in swaddling clothes and lying in a manger.

ESTHER: Voices? What voices?

ELAM: That's just it. We don't know.

ISAAC: What happened?

JOASH: We were watching the sheep. Then suddenly in the darkness light began to glow and it grew brighter and brighter.

ELAM: Until it was brighter than the brightest sunlight!

JOASH: Then there was this voice.

MERAB: A voice?

ELAM: Maybe one, maybe several!

JOASH: Anyway we understood the words. They said for us to come to Bethlehem, and we'd find the Messiah in a manger in swaddling clothes.

ESTHER (*rising*): Messiah?

ELAM: That's right. Then we heard words, like a chorus, saying "Glory to God."

JOASH: Then the light went away. And the sounds.

ELAM: The only sounds were the sheep moving restlessly.

(*Leah and Jephthah enter left.*)

JEPHTHAH: What's all the noise?

LEAH: Joash! Elam! Why are you here at this hour?

JEPHTHAH: Elam, I told you to keep Joash away from Merab!

ELAM (*excited still*): Listen, Jephthah.

JEPHTHAH (*harshly*): No, you listen! Both of you get out of here right now! (*He goes at Elam in a threatening manner. Esther comes between.*)

ESTHER: Wait, Jephthah! Listen! This has nothing to do with Merab!

JEPHTHAH (*looks at Elam*): Is this so?

ELAM: That's right! Something strange happened tonight. We've had some sort of visitation out on that hillside.

JOASH: Voices told us to come see a newborn baby in a manger here.

ELAM: So Joash and I left Caleb with the sheep and ran all the way.

JEPHTHAH: I don't believe it.

ELAM: If I hadn't heard and seen it myself, probably I wouldn't believe it either.

JOASH: It's true! There was the light and the voices telling us to come see the baby!

ELAM: That's so. Now, where is he?

JEPHTHAH: There's no baby here.

LEAH (*impatiently*): Oh, Jephthah! There has to be a baby! Don't you see Esther and Merab out here and not in the stable? So the baby has come. What is it, Esther?

ESTHER: A beautiful boy.

ELAM: The Messiah! Just as we heard! We want to see him!

LEAH: In the middle of the night?

ESTHER: Why not? Babies are always turning night into day. Come on, I'll take you.

(*Esther and shepherds leave right. Merab sits on the well bench. Leah and Jephthah start for stable and then stop.*)

MERAB: This is the first time I ever saw a baby born. It is sort of wonderful, isn't it? He's so little. To think he'll grow up into a man some day. I hope I have many sons!

ISAAC: Don't be in a hurry.

JEPHTHAH (*glumly*): Leah, do you realize that woman has to stay here a few days more? Probably can't pay for an extended stay. So what now?

LEAH: See? If you'd turned them away, they'd be someone else's responsibility. We can't just put them out now.

JEPHTHAH: I know. What would people say?

ISAAC: When the census is over and people go home, the little house of Eliakim ben Joshua will be empty. Eliakim will not return from visiting his son until after the harvest. These Nazarenes could stay there.

LEAH: Good! Then Eliakim can worry about the pay!

(*Obed comes from the right. He confronts Jephthah and Leah. Merab looks on bewildered by his manner.*)

OBED: Jephthah!

JEPHTHAH: What now?

OBED: Listen, Merab! Jephthah, I've changed my mind. Tell her!

JEPHTHAH (*blustering*): You don't know what you're saying! What's come over you?

OBED (*grimly*): Tell her, Jephthah. Or I will!

JEPHTHAH: You'd throw away your chances? Oh, no, I don't believe you.

OBED: I may regret this later, but for now I mean it. Tell her!

MERAB: What is it, Obed? Tell me what?

LEAH (*nervously*): Oh, nothing, child. Just nothing. You'd better get to sleep, Obed! I—I'll need you early in the morning.

OBED: Well? You or me?

JEPHTHAH: Now, Obed, be reasonable!

MERAB (*impatient*): Reasonable about what?

(*Esther and the shepherds return, realize something is happening. Elam and Joash stop stage right. Esther comes to Merab by the well.*)

MERAB (*bewildered*): Mother?

ESTHER: What is it, Merab? What's wrong?

MERAB: I don't know, Obed?

OBED: Very well, Jephthah. Time's up!

JEPHTHAH (*angrily*): All right, all right! I'll tell her! You keep out of it!

LEAH (*wailing*): Oh, Jephthah!

JEPHTHAH: Hush, Leah! What has to be has to be.

(*Jephthah assumes a hearty, paternal manner.*)

JEPHTHAH: Well, Esther, the time has come to tell you and Merab something—something to your—uh—benefit. Yes, your benefit. You must understand I have kept it from you for the best of reasons, the very best of reasons!

OBED (*grimly*): Get on with it!

JEPHTHAH: My whole purpose was to protect you. That's it! I wanted to protect you, just as my dear brother would have wished. In these years I was waiting for just the right time to tell you.

OBED: Get it over with, Jephthah!

JEPHTHAH: Well, the truth is, Joel left you money in my keeping.

ESTHER (*still not understanding*): Which you have kept carefully, I am sure.

JEPHTHAH: Of course!

OBED: Go on! Tell it all! If you can't say it, I can! Esther, you needn't have worked for Jephthah all these years for nothing.

And Merab has an ample dowry. Your husband left you well off! See, Jephthah? That wasn't so hard!

JEPHTHAH (*miserably*): Uh—no.

ESTHER; You mean? We needn't? All these years? (*Appalled.*) But *why?* Oh, Jephthah!

JEPHTHAH (*defensively*): It was for your own good!

OBED: Ha!

JEPHTHAH (*defensively*): You and Merab were all alone! You needed a man to care for you.

ESTHER (*with pity*): Oh, Jephthah!

MERAB (*accusingly*): Uncle Jephthah, you knew Joash and I needed that dowry!

(*Joash takes Merab by the hand.*)

ELAM (*gratefully*): Well, this certainly changes things! Thanks to Obed.

(*Merab takes Obed's hand and presses it against her cheek.*)

MERAB: How can I ever thank you? My friend! My dear friend.

OBED: Well, that's better than nothing. Not much, but a little better.

JOASH: Thank you, Obed. We owe you a lot.

OBED: I think so, too.

ELAM: We'll have to hear more at another time. Joash, we must return to the flock. Caleb is alone. We have real news for him. We found the baby, the Messiah. And the way is open for your marriage. God bless you, Obed. Come, Joash! (*He leaves.*)

JOASH (*to Merab*): I'll be back tomorrow. Here, not the grove. I will think of you every minute! (*He leaves left.*)

OBED: Well, that's that. Jephthah, you have an accounting for tomorrow. Sleep well!

JEPHTHAH: You're a fool, Obed. Come, Leah. I know I won't sleep a wink! (*They go left.*)

MERAB: Obed, how can I ever thank you? You are truly wonderful!

OBED (*frankly*): Yes, I guess I am. You know, this is the first time I ever really did anything for anybody! Anything important, that is.

ISAAC: Feels pretty good, doesn't it?

OBED: Right now. Of course, there's tomorrow.

ESTHER: Tomorrow isn't far off. I will stay with Mary until morning. Merab, go to bed, There's a busy day ahead. Sleep well!

MERAB (*embracing her*): You, too. Good-night, dear Obed! Sleep well, Isaac. (*She leaves left.*)

ESTHER: Pull your cloak around you, Isaac. The night is cool. Obed! Dear Obed! (*She touches his arm lovingly and then goes right.*)

(*Obed looks after her a moment, then sits on the well bench. He breaks the silence.*)

OBED: She never would have forgotten Joash, would she?

ISAAC: No, Merab is that kind of woman. She gives her heart once for life.

OBED: I really knew that. But I wanted to believe she'd forget in time and come to care for me.

ISAAC: I know.

OBED (*cheerfully*): Well, I'll get over it. I'm not that constant!

ISAAC: Good!

OBED (*wistfully*): She'll be happy?

ISAAC: As happy as people ever are in this world . . . Obed, why?

OBED: Why, what?

ISAAC: Why did you tell? I wouldn't have betrayed you.

OBED: I know.

ISAAC: It isn't my place to interfere in the lives of others.

OBED: I know.

ISAAC: Then why?

OBED (*thoughtfully*): I don't know. Isaac, I really don't know. I'm no saint. I grab what I can and hold on. I had everything going my way. Everything was under control.

ISAAC: Yet, you let her go. When did you change your mind?

OBED (*thinking*): It had to be—it was in the stable. That's it! That's when it was! Isaac, it was that baby! I went in, and there he was. Just a little newborn baby. I looked at him, and he was kicking his little feet. Then I looked in his eyes, and he looked back! For a long time he looked back!

ISAAC: Obed, little new babies can't see.

OBED: This one can! He looked back at me and he stopped kicking and was still. Then his mother broke the spell. She picked him up and held him close. I started moving hay to make her more comfortable.

ISAAC: Stacking hay?

OBED: No, just making her bed a little softer. I don't know why. I just did it. Then Elam and Joash came in. When they were telling her about the voices they heard, I looked at that baby and then at Joash. That's when I knew. So I came outside and you saw the rest.

ISAAC: You think what Elam and Joash heard is true? Is this baby the Messiah? Is he something special?

OBED: I don't know about the Messiah part. But there *is* something special about that baby. Really something special. I wish you could see him.

ISAAC: Well, why not?

OBED: You mean you will?

ISAAC: Will they be asleep?

OBED: Probably not, with all that's happened.

ISAAC: Then, if you'll help me, I'll go see him now.

(*Obed helps him stand, gives him his crutch and supports him from the other side. About halfway, Isaac begins to talk.*)

ISAAC: Obed, you know what?

OBED: What?

ISAAC: I know something about you you don't know.

OBED: What's that?

ISAAC: If there hadn't been a dowry for Merab, she'd have had one anyway.

OBED: From whom?

ISAAC: From you. You'd have given her what you've saved these years.

OBED: I would?

ISAAC: Yes, you would.

OBED (*thoughtfully, after pause*): I guess I would at that!

(*They leave right.*)

2
The Tree

Cast

Philip Hodges, the father
Susan, the mother
Larry, the sixteen-year-old son
Beth, the fourteen-year-old daughter
George, a delivery boy, at least sixteen.

Setting

The setting is the living room of the Hodges' home. If space or use of the church worship center is a problem, don't try a real setting. Instead use: two folding chairs side by side, one chair apart, small table for phone and phone book, a table for the small tree and crèche. The audience's imagination will furnish the room.

Props

Props needed are small, scrawny Christmas tree with few branches or needles, ample tree decorations, Beth's school books, two folding TV tables, a phone that can ring, phone book with yellow pages, tape of carols and player offstage, small radio, small crèche.

(*Beth enters, drops school books, flops rebelliously on a chair. Then Larry follows. Both are angry.*)

BETH: I hope you're satisfied!

LARRY: Not particularly! That guy's older than I am and a lot meaner! He could be real trouble.

BETH: Then why did you butt in? He likes me! It was none of your business.

LARRY: When my stupid fourteen-year-old sister—

BETH: Nearly fifteen!

LARRY (*louder*): Not for six months! When my stupid fourteen-year-old sister starts getting mixed up with Butch Henderson, then I'm making it my business!

BETH: You're only sixteen yourself. You're not my father!

LARRY: No, I'm not! But I'm the nearest thing to a father around here right now.

BETH: Ha!

LARRY: You're gonna do like I say! You hear me?

BETH: I hear you. But it doesn't mean anything.

LARRY: No? What if I call Father and tell him you're about to get into real trouble?

BETH: He won't care.

LARRY: Oh, no? I can make him listen when I tell him Butch Henderson is bad news.

BETH: The older girls all think he's something extra. You should hear them.

LARRY: What older girls? Not the nice ones. They're too smart. They know he's a no-good. Beth, he's nearly twenty and too stupid to graduate!

BETH: That's not true!

LARRY: Of course it's true. Besides being a rat, he's stupid. And I meant what I said. He'd better stay away from you.

BETH: Why should I listen to you?

LARRY: Because I'm sticking my neck out for you! That guy could mop up the floor with me if he had a mind to.

BETH (*slumps in chair*): I wish he would! I hate everybody! I ought to run away! I'm so miserable!

LARRY (*sits beside her, looks at her a moment*): I know. It's rough, Sis.

BETH (*miserably*): Everything is a mess. Nobody cares. I wish I were dead.

LARRY (*trying to sound cheerful*): It's not that bad. You've got Mother and me.

BETH: Oh, great.

LARRY: Hang in there. You'll see. It'll be okay.

BETH: Larry, before the divorce, things used to be different. I don't see why Mother had to get a divorce. Why did everything have to change?

LARRY: Oh, lots of reasons. I don't understand them all myself.

BETH: She could have let things stay the same if she'd wanted to!

LARRY: She didn't think so.

BETH (*wistfully*): I even miss the fighting!

LARRY (*ruefully*): There were some lulus, weren't there?

BETH (*rises and walks about*): I don't understand anything. At least the way it used to be, Father came home sometime. Even if he was always busy in his study and we hardly ever saw him. Once I remember, when I was about nine, we all went on that business trip with him to Mexico. Remember?

LARRY (*laughs*): Yeah, and you got sick and Mother had to stay in the hotel with you while I went with Father. Not that it mattered, because all I did was sit in the waiting rooms of a zillion offices while he tended to business. I got so sick of looking at magazines all printed in Spanish that I couldn't read! Beth, you know what?

BETH: What?

LARRY: I never told this to anyone before. I guess I was ashamed. Father *forgot* me one day in one of those offices! I guess he went out another way. I didn't see him go.

BETH (*dismayed*): He didn't! How *could* he? Just left you?

LARRY: Forgot all about me.

BETH (*sits beside him*): What did you do?

LARRY: Well, when everyone in the place left, I went out and started walking. I kept asking where the hotel was, but no one could understand me. Just before dark, I saw a store with a sign, "English Spoken." There was a little man in there not much taller than I was and I was only eleven. He understood me and pointed the way to the hotel.

BETH: I'll bet Mother and Father were frantic.

LARRY: No, they hadn't even missed me.

BETH (*sympathetically*): Oh, Larry!

LARRY: When I walked in, Father said: "Larry, you're late for supper. If you can't be around when you are supposed to be, I won't take you on another trip!" What's more, he didn't. Never again.

BETH: Oh, Larry, I'm sorry!

LARRY (*minimizing*): It doesn't matter. Now, Beth, let's talk about Butch Henderson. He's *no good.* He's the one who's been selling stuff at school—pills, grass, maybe the hard stuff. He gets booze for the kids, too.

BETH: He hasn't tried to sell me any.

LARRY: Beth, listen. I know you think you're old enough to take care of yourself. But I'm older than you are, and I'm old enough to know I'm *not* old enough to take care of myself!

BETH (*intrigued*): Really?

LARRY: Really.

BETH: Butch asked me to a party at his house Christmas day.

LARRY: Forget it. What's the matter with getting back with your old church friends? There's Billy and Grace and the girl with the red hair—what's her name?

BETH: Marsha.

LARRY: Marsha. And those Johnson kids. What happened to them?

BETH (*rises and moves away*): I—I just—well, after all the mess and the divorce—oh, I got tired of their saying they were sorry!

LARRY: We aren't the only ones with divorced parents. Maybe they *were* sorry. Those Johnson kids—why their parents divorced when they were real little.

BETH: I didn't think of that.

LARRY: It dies down. My friends don't mention it now. Beth, come with me Sunday.

BETH (*glumly*): Oh, I don't know. Mother doesn't go any more.

LARRY: Maybe she feels like you do. Maybe she thinks people will think she's failed some way.

BETH: It's a mess, isn't it? It's all Mother's fault!

LARRY (*goes to her*): Don't say that, Beth. She's really trying. Since Father left, she tries to take care of things here and work at a job, too.

BETH: She doesn't half do anything! Why can't she keep a job, Larry? She must have gotten eight jobs and the longest lasted two weeks!

LARRY: Beth, you ought to understand Mother better than anyone else does, because you are so much alike.

BETH: I am not!

LARRY: Remember you promised to take my jacket to the cleaner this morning and to pick it up again on your way home?

BETH (*contritely*): Oh, I forgot! Shall I go now?

LARRY: Never mind. I took it by. I'll get it later. See, Beth? You and Mother are sort of irresponsible.

BETH: I don't mean to be.

LARRY: Neither does Mother. Now when people are paying Mother to do a job, they expect her to *do* it. But Mother forgets or she sees someone who needs some help. Or someone stops her with a question. Then she'll forget all about what she was supposed to be doing. In business that won't work out. So they let her go.

BETH (*sits, thinking*): I know she's not stupid.

LARRY (*sits by her*): No, she's not. It took me a while to understand. I think she's just geared to a different tempo. The things most people consider important don't matter to her so much as the people themselves. She really digs people.

BETH: Why, Larry, I never saw that before. Now that I think about it, when I was a little girl, she always had time to stop whatever she was doing to listen to me. She really listened. Which is more than anyone else in this family ever did.

LARRY: I'm listening.

BETH: But when I was little, you were always out playing. Father was always too busy to pay any attention to me. You know what I remember most about Father? I remember him coming home and quarreling with Mother with never so much as a hello to me!

LARRY (*remembering*): He used to get very upset because she didn't do things she'd promised to do. Probably because she was listening to you!

BETH (*amused*): Do you suppose that was it?

LARRY: I wouldn't be surprised. She felt it was more important to be with you, and he felt she was irresponsible. Beth, you know what? If I ever get married and if I ever have children, I'm going to spend some time with *them*. They're going to know they are important.

BETH (*laughs*): Even if your jacket doesn't get to the cleaner?

LARRY (*laughs*): Even that.

BETH: Oh, Larry! (*She gives him a quick hug.*)

LARRY (*embarrassed*): Aw, now, Beth! Come on, let's see what we can fix for supper.

BETH (*as they rise*): Provided Mother went to the store today. She was going to see about a job. She said she'd bring the groceries when she came back.

LARRY: Don't I hear her now?

(*Susan enters, without the groceries*)

SUSAN: Hi, you two! Oh, what good news I have!

LARRY: You found a job.

SUSAN: How did you know? I start this evening!

LARRY: This evening?

BETH: Where?

LARRY: Doing what?

SUSAN (*happily*): The florist on Fifth Street—Breemer's! I deliver flowers and plants for him! Isn't it fortunate your father left me the station wagon?

LARRY (*disapproving*): You have to use *your* car?

SUSAN (*happily*): Oh, yes. Mr. Breemer says he has so many orders at Christmas he has to hire extra help. I got the job because I had the car. Wasn't it lucky?

BETH (*disappointed*): The job only lasts through Christmas!

SUSAN (*optimistically*): Well, yes. But something else will turn up.

BETH: Did you bring the groceries, Mother?

SUSAN (*guiltily*): Oh, dear! I forgot all about the groceries! I thought you'd be so pleased about the job. I'll go back right now.

BETH: Never mind. We'll find something for supper.

SUSAN: Larry, before I forget, the pastor called this morning and asked if I'd have the young people's Christmas party here. If I felt *up* to it. I'm really ashamed of how neglectful I've been. The church isn't responsible for our troubles. So I said yes. But now with this job. . . .

LARRY: I'll call Mrs. Bateman. She's chairman of the committee.

Don't worry about it Mother. She'll find someone.

SUSAN (*relieved*): Oh, thank you! I just never seem to get caught up.

BETH: Your trouble is, Father did so many things for you, Mother.

SUSAN: Not really, Beth. He just passed them on to Miss Cummings. Of all the things I miss since your Father left, I think I miss Hilda Cummings most. Now there is a capable woman. She'd never forget the groceries and leave her children starving on her doorstep!

LARRY (*laughs*): It's not that bad, Mother.

SUSAN: Beth, have you seen my green blouse? It's just the thing to wear delivering flowers!

BETH: It's in the clothes hamper with the dirty clothes.

SUSAN: Oh, dear! I meant to wash this week.

(*Susan leaves, then returns immediately.*)

SUSAN: Larry, I forgot. Go look in the car.

(*She leaves. Larry leaves. Beth picks up her books and puts them on the phone table. Larry returns with a scrawny little Christmas tree.*)

BETH: What on earth is *that?*

LARRY (*dismayed*): Mother!

(*Susan enters.*)

SUSAN (*happily*): Oh, you found it! Mr. Breemer *gave* it to me. Wasn't that lucky? Now we won't have to buy a tree! Aren't you proud of me? Mr. Breemer couldn't sell this one.

BETH: I'm not surprised. Mother, that's the worst tree I ever saw!

SUSAN: Oh, it's not so bad. We'll get the ornaments on and then you'll see.

(*She leaves.*)

BETH: Oh, Larry!

LARRY (*placing tree on small table*): Brace up, Sis! As Mom said, at least it's free.

(*Their father, Philip, enters.*)

PHILIP: Hello there.

BETH: Father!

LARRY: What are you doing here?

PHILIP: I'm not welcome?

BETH: Of course you are welcome, Father.

PHILIP: The door was standing open. I did knock, but no one heard me apparently. Well—ah—you both look good.

LARRY: You, too, Father. We haven't seen you lately. Sometimes I look for you in church. Sundays, that is.

PHILIP: I've been tied up weekends.

LARRY (*uncomfortably*): Won't you sit down?

PHILIP: No, I can't stay. Just came by for my skis.

BETH (*blankly*): Skis?

PHILIP: Yes, *skis*. I'm going to Colorado for Christmas.

BETH (*disappointed*): We thought maybe. . . .

PHILIP (*interrupting*): I see you are getting ready to decorate a tree. (*sarcastically*) That is a tree, I suppose?

BETH: It's a crummy tree!

LARRY (*defensively*): It'll be okay when I get through with it. At least it didn't cost anything.

PHILIP (*sharply*): What's that? I give your mother enough money to buy a decent tree if you want one!

LARRY (*irked*): No, thanks! We'll manage.

(*Susan enters.*)

SUSAN: Oh! Philip. I didn't hear you.

PHILIP (*false heartiness*): Hello, Susan. You're looking well.

SUSAN: Oh, I am. I have a new job!

PHILIP: That's good. Well, I won't keep you. Just stopped by for my skis.

SUSAN (*blankly*): Skis?

PHILIP (*annoyed*): What's this about my skis? I do own some.

SUSAN: I'm just surprised. That's all. I gave you those skis four years ago. They were for the vacation we didn't take. Remember?

PHILIP (*irked*): Now don't start that! Is it my fault I was busy?

SUSAN: Probably. However there was no vacation. Then or any other.

PHILIP (*annoyed*): I was *busy!* That was something you never understood.

SUSAN (*angry*): You were always busy, Phil. You never had any time for us, did you? You should never have had a wife and children!

PHILIP (*ominously*): Now, Susan!

SUSAN: You know, I could have understood another woman better.

PHILIP (*angry*): That's a fine thing to say before your children!

SUSAN: I might have done something about another woman! But a man who is in love with his business—

PHILIP: Beth, Larry, go out into the kitchen!

LARRY (*he sits and pulls Beth down by him*): Why? We've heard it all before.

PHILIP: Then if you'll give me the skis, I'll go!

SUSAN (*angry*): I don't know where they are, but I'll go look so you can go!

PHILIP: I might have known you wouldn't be able to locate them! I'll look myself!

(*He stalks out and she follows.*)

LARRY (*serenely*): I hope he breaks his leg.

BETH (*glumly*): I wish I could go skiing. I wish I could go any where, even Butch Henderson's Christmas party.

LARRY: Lay off Butch Henderson!

BETH: Christmas! I hate Christmas!

LARRY: Go get the Christmas decorations! We'll see what we can do with this tree.

BETH: Go get them yourself! You heard Father. He thinks it's a crummy tree too. We always had a nice tree when he was here.

LARRY: Thanks to Miss Cummings.

(*Susan and Philip return.*)

PHILIP (*angry*): Why can't you remember where you put them?

SUSAN (*angry*): Because I can't!

PHILIP: You probably gave them away.

SUSAN: I would remember that.

PHILIP: Susan, you are just as irresponsible as ever!

SUSAN: I'm not Miss Cummings, if that's what you mean.

PHILIP: At least she knows where she puts things!

SUSAN: She never forgets anything.

PHILIP: If she did I'd fire her!

SUSAN: Like you fired me?

PHILIP: Susan, you know the divorce was your idea!

SUSAN: The divorce was the final formality. This never was your home. That office is your home, with Miss Cummings as the obedient slave!

PHILIP: Leave Hilda out of this!

SUSAN: Don't worry. She'll never let you down. You'll never have to fire her.

PHILIP: This conversation is in poor taste.

SUSAN: Is it? With both of you worshiping that business, and both of you so efficient, I'm surprised you don't marry her!

PHILIP (*stiffly*): Miss Cummings is fifteen years older than I am.

SUSAN: What difference does that make? You never look at a *wife* anyway!

PHILIP (*coldly*): Susan, don't exaggerate!

SUSAN: Exaggerate? About a wife and children you didn't want or need? I'm remembering the fishing trip we didn't take, the father-son and father-daughter banquets you didn't attend, the church where you didn't worship because of business. You married a wife and you sired two children and that was that. Period. Were we part of some finished business schedule, Philip?

PHILIP: Don't be ridiculous! Didn't I always support all of you? Larry, did you ever lack for anything?

LARRY (*embarrassed*): Well—I—

PHILIP: Of course not! And you Beth, didn't you always have all you needed?

SUSAN (*almost shouting*): I'll *buy* you some skis if I can't find those!

PHILIP (*coldly*): Don't bother. I'll buy my own.

LARRY: Father, aren't you going to be here at all for Christmas?

SUSAN: It won't be the first time.

BETH: I don't care! I won't be here either. I'm going to a party at Butch Henderson's.

LARRY (*jumping up*): No, you're not! Father, listen! Help me. Beth's getting mixed up with this guy at school. Father, he's no good!

SUSAN (*surprised*): What's this?

PHILIP: Beth, what have you to say?

BETH (*jumping up*): At least he thinks enough of me to invite me to his Christmas party!

LARRY: Some party that will be. Father, he's too old for her, and he's the one who sells stuff at school.

PHILIP: Stuff?

LARRY: Pills, grass, drugs.

PHILIP (*indignant*): You mean that school still hasn't stopped such things? Do they know about this fellow?

LARRY: A lot of the students do.

PHILIP: Why doesn't somebody do something?

LARRY: Oh, Father!

PHILIP: I simply don't understand such an attitude! All right, Beth. You stay away from all that stuff. Do you hear me?

BETH: I hear you.

PHILIP: That's a good girl. Now, I must go.

LARRY (*desperately*): Father! Don't you see? She's not going to pay any attention to you. Mom, say something!

SUSAN (*uncertainly*): Beth, you heard your father. Listen to him.

PHILIP: Beth is a sensible girl.

LARRY: No, she isn't. She's like Mother.

BETH: Oh, shut up, Larry!

LARRY: She's gullible and she needs someone to look after her.

SUSAN: What a thing to say! Didn't I go out and get a new job?

PHILIP: Larry, watch what you say. Beth, you heard me. Now

I'm busy and can't come out and referee arguments. You've just got to settle it among yourselves. I must go. I'm seeing a client at dinner. Susan, call me when you find those skis. Good-bye. Merry Christmas!

(*He leaves.*)

LARRY (*sarcastically after him*): And a merry to you, too, Father!

SUSAN (*touching his arm*): Larry, I'm sorry.

LARRY: What for?

SUSAN: I'm just sorry.

BETH: I'm hungry.

SUSAN: Let's go see what we can find for supper, Beth.

BETH: Okay.

(*They leave. Larry goes off and returns with a generous box of tree decorations. He looks at the scrawny tree on the table and begins. Time this decoration so that it comes out right in the script. Let him work long enough for Beth's return to seem reasonable. When Beth brings in the crèche at the end, the tree should be heavily covered and look quite good.*)

BETH: Guess what we're having for supper.

LARRY: TV dinners.

BETH: How did you know?

LARRY: Stands to reason.

BETH: Mom likes the salisbury steak. You can have the fried chicken. I'll take the roast beef. Don't say I'm not good to you sometime.

LARRY: I won't. If you'll promise not to see Butch Henderson any more. Beth, say you didn't mean what you told Father.

BETH: Well, maybe.

(*Susan calls from offstage.*)

SUSAN: Larry! What time is it? This clock says noon and my

watch says four.

LARRY (*looks at his watch*): It's six-fifteen.

SUSAN: *What?*

LARRY (*louder*): Six-fifteen!

SUSAN: Oh, dear! (*she enters hurriedly.*) I've got to go!

BETH: But your supper—

SUSAN: There isn't time! I'm already overdue at Breemer's to deliver plants. Oh, where has the time gone? Where is my purse and the car keys?

(*She rushes off again.*)

BETH (*calls out*): Look on the sink!

(*Susan rushes back, purse and keys in hand.*)

SUSAN: Now how did they get there? I'll be home as soon as possible. Oh, good! You're decorating the tree. 'Bye, kids!

(*She leaves.*)

LARRY: How *did* her purse and keys get on the sink?

BETH: Who knows? Well, you can have the salisbury steak, too, if the chicken isn't enough. Where's the star for the top?

LARRY: It's here. It goes on last.

BETH (*picking through ornaments*): Whatever happened to the pink angel we used to have when I was little? We did have one, didn't we? I know I remember a pink angel from somewhere.

LARRY: I broke it.

BETH: Accidentally?

LARRY: No.

BETH: On *purpose?*

LARRY: Yep.

BETH: Why?

LARRY: Oh, Father was off on one of his trips. He promised to be home for Christmas. Then he called and said he couldn't make it. So I got the kitchen ladder and took the angel off the top of the tree and broke it.

BETH: But why?

LARRY: Oh, I don't know. I just did.

BETH: Heavens! What did Mother say?

LARRY: Nothing. Later on she said why not have a star on top of the tree next year. So we did. Do you think it would help if I got some pieces of branches and wired into these bare spots?

BETH: Frankly, I don't think anything will help that tree. Want to give up?

LARRY: No! I'm going to make this look like a Christmas tree ought to look if it takes all night!

BETH: If it's going to take that long, you need to keep your strength up. Why don't I put TV tables in here? Then we can watch TV while we eat.

LARRY: TV tables for TV dinners to watch TV.

(*She goes off and returns with two folding TV tables. She opens them as she talks.*)

BETH: I'm going to learn to cook. Really cook, you know. With herbs and spices and all that stuff. Then no more TV dinners.

LARRY: Who's going to teach you? Not Mom.

BETH: I'll take courses at school next year. Just you wait and see!

LARRY: When you are the world's greatest cook, invite me over, will you? Now, what I like is rare two-inch steak, potatoes au gratin, tossed salad with a really good Roquefort dressing. Then either strawberries or peaches with French vanilla ice cream. But if I have to wait until you are the world's greatest cook, I'll be able to eat only boiled rice and milk!

Beth: Ha! Little do you know! I am a determined woman.

Larry: If you are so determined, don't you smell something?

Beth (*cries out*): The TV dinners!

(*She runs off. Then there's a hammering as if on an outside door. Larry goes and a frightened youth enters.*)

George: Where's Mr. Hodges? I gotta see Mr. Hodges!

Larry: My father doesn't live here any more. I'm Larry.

George: I guess Mr. Breemer didn't know about Mr. Hodges.

Larry: What's the matter?

George: It's Mrs. Hodges!

(*Beth enters.*)

Beth: Larry! What's wrong?

Larry: It's about Mother.

Beth: What about Mother?

George: That's what I'm trying to tell you. There's been an accident. She's in the hospital!

Beth and Larry (*frightened*): *Hospital?*

George: Northside Hospital, just a few blocks from here. Mr. Breemer said your phone wasn't working and sent me with the van to take you—Mr. Hodges, that is—to the hospital. Her station wagon is a mess!

Beth (*frightened*): Oh, Larry, is she going to die?

Larry: Is she badly hurt?

George (*nervously*): I don't know. The ambulance took her to Northside Hospital. She was unconscious. The guy in the truck that hit her didn't get a scratch!

Larry: Beth, you try to get Father.

Beth: No! I want to go with you!

George: Your phone's not working.

(*Larry picks up the phone and listens.*)

LARRY: Seems okay now. Beth, I'll go with—say, what's your name?

GEORGE: George.

LARRY: I'll go with George and you find Father.

BETH (*pleading*): Let me go, too. I don't know where Father is.

LARRY: Try Miss Cummings. Her number is by the phone. Tell Father I've gone with George. I'll call you from the hospital. Now, don't worry!

BETH: Please let me go!

LARRY: Somebody has to find Father. I'm counting on you, Beth.

(*He and George leave. Beth looks for phone number and dials. Waits, hangs up.*)

BETH: Maybe I dialed wrong. (*Dials again*) Please answer, Miss Cummings! (*Waits. Hangs up.*) (*desperately*) Now what? Oh, God, don't let anything happen to Mother! please don't! (*sniffles*) I mustn't cry. Where could Father be? (*remembers*) Oh! He said he was seeing a client at dinner! *Where?* Raburns? (*She looks up the number in the phone book and dials.*) Please be there!

BETH: Hello. This is Beth Hodges and I'm trying to get in touch with Philip Hodges. Is he there? . . . Does he have a reservation? . . . He doesn't? Well, if he comes in later, will you tell him there's been an accident and Mrs. Hodges has been taken to Northside Hospital? . . . Thank you.

(*She hangs up and begins looking in the book again.*)

BETH: The Angus! Maybe he's there. Here it is. (*She dials.*) . . . Hello, this is Beth Hodges. I'm trying to find my father. It's an emergency. His name is Philip Hodges . . . You haven't seen him? Will you look to see if he has a reservation? . . . Well, thank you. (*She hangs up and looks in the book again.*) Now what? The Crestview! Maybe he's there. (*She dials.*) . . . Crestview? Is Philip Hodges there this evening? . . . Will you look in your reservations? . . . This is his daughter. If he happens to come in or call, will you please tell him to call Northside Hospital? Mrs. Hodges has been in an accident. Thank you.

(*She hangs up and looks at the book.*)

BETH: Now where? Oh, I can't think! Father, where are you? . . . The yellow pages! (*She turns in the book.*) Restaurants, restaurants . . . Here they are: Abernathy's Cafeteria, All night Diner, Big Top, Call-It-Inn, Carrington's—Carrington's! We ate there once. (*Dials*) Hello, Carrington's? . . . Is there a Philip Hodges there tonight? . . . Can't you ask? . . . But this is an emergency! . . . Please, sir! He's my father and my mother's been in an accident! She's in Northside Hospital! You won't? It's the policy? Yes, I heard you. I just hope this never happens to you! (*She hangs up.*) Oh, Mother! Why doesn't Larry call? (*She looks in the book and then dials.*)

BETH: Northside? This is Beth Hodges. My mother was brought in a little while ago and I want to know how she is . . . a car accident, yes . . . the emergency room? . . . Do you know how badly she is hurt? . . . But . . . Yes, I know. I'll call later.

(*She hangs up. Then she walks over to the tree and touches the tip of a branch gently. The phone rings. She runs to answer.*)

BETH: Hello! . . . Oh, Larry! What about Mother? . . . Why wouldn't they let you in the emergency room? . . . Why is she still unconscious? . . . What? . . . No, I haven't found him yet . . . Miss Cummings isn't home. I've been calling places he might be. Remember he said he was taking a client to dinner? . . . Why can't I come down? . . . I left messages all around. If he calls, I'll tell him. All right. Call me the minute she's conscious . . . Okay.

(*She hangs up and looks at the phone. Then she begins to cry, but she doesn't want to cry, so she tries to occupy herself.*

She begins to work on the tree. She turns on the small radio.)

RADIO: This is station KMUS, your good music station. Tonight, in honor of the season, we are playing Christmas carols from around the world.

(*Carols begin softly. Beth stands and listens a moment, then resumes work on the tree, slowly. She stops to blow her nose now and then and sniffle. The phone rings. She answers quickly.*)

BETH: Hello! . . . Larry? Yes, what about Mother? . . . Why is she still unconscious? Oh, Larry! . . . He *is?* . . . When did he get there? . . . They *did?* . . . Yes, I'm all right . . . Call me when you know anything. 'Bye.

(*She hangs up, thinks a moment.*)

BETH: God, please let her be all right. Please don't let her die! Not at *Christmas*. Please. Thank you for finding Father.

(*She stands with head bowed, wiping her eyes. Then she goes to the radio and listens, turning up the volume. After a moment she turns it down again and goes to phone. She looks up a number and dials.*)

BETH: Carrington's? This is Beth Hodges. I called a while ago trying to locate my father . . . Then you are the one I talked to? . . . Well, I just want to thank you for getting the message to him. Also I want to apologize for being rude to you . . . Yes, he reached the hospital all right . . . No, my mother is still unconscious. That's all I know . . . Thank you, and Merry Christmas to you, too!

(*She hangs up. Then she turns up the radio. She puts away the TV tables, one at a time, slowly. She resumes work on the tree. In a few minutes Larry and Philip enter.*)

BETH (*frightened, goes to them*): Father! Larry! Why are you here? Is Mother—?

PHILIP: Right after Larry called you, the doctor came and said she was in a natural sleep now.

BETH: Did you talk to her?

PHILIP: No, she hasn't really waked up at all.

BETH: Then why are you here?

LARRY: The doctor sent us home. They gave her sedatives for pain. He said she'd sleep for hours; and we couldn't do anything there, except get in the way.

BETH (*upset*): But she's alone!

PHILIP (*comforting her*): But there are nurses and doctors there, Beth. They will take good care of her.

BETH: Let me go and just stay near so she'll know someone is there.

PHILIP (*firmly*): No, Beth. She won't know you're there. Be sensible.

BETH: I don't want to be sensible!

LARRY: What you want is to go back to six-fifteen.

PHILIP: Six-fifteen?

LARRY: When Mother left for Breemers.

PHILIP: That silly little job!

LARRY: Maybe it wasn't much of a job, but she was proud of getting it herself.

PHILIP: I will never understand your mother. Susan knows she doesn't have to work. I will always provide for her and you children. My business is more than adequate to give us all a good living.

LARRY: It should be. You've devoted enough time to it.

PHILIP (*with pride*): That's why I've made such a success of it. Your mother never understood that time is the price of success.

LARRY: Maybe she doesn't think of it as success.

PHILIP (*surprised*): Are you saying she thinks I am a failure? (*When he doesn't answer*) Well, Larry?

LARRY: Father, I don't want to quarrel with you. Especially about Mother.

PHILIP: No, let's have it out! Whenever I am around you and Beth I detect an undercurrent of criticism. What is it? I insist you tell me!

LARRY (*reluctantly*): Father, no one denies you are a success in business. But as a father and husband. . . .

PHILIP: I'm a failure? You think I'm a failure?

BETH: Oh, Father!

PHILIP: Keep out of this, Beth. Let him speak. So I'm a failure, am I? My son calls me a failure?

LARRY: That's it! Am I your son? Or just another dependent? Other guys I know have a real thing going with their fathers. It's not clothes or money. It's being together and liking each other. It's taking time to talk and see things together, and knowing your father is the best friend you have.

BETH: Larry, please.

PHILIP: No, Beth, let him speak. I think I'm being blamed for being industrious. Is it a virtue to be a failure?

LARRY: Just let it go.

PHILIP: Are you afraid to speak up?

BETH: No, he's not! Larry's *good!* And he's *brave!* He stood up to Butch Henderson even though Butch is lots bigger. You're a terrible father, and I hate you!

PHILIP: Beth!

BETH: I hate you for never being here. You don't care anything about us. Why did you marry Mother? Why did you let us be born? If Mother dies, I won't live with you! I'd rather die first!

LARRY: Beth, don't.

BETH: I don't care! I'm sorry for the things I said about Mother!

At least we know she loves us.

PHILIP (*awkwardly*): I—I love you, Beth.

BETH: No, you don't. You just love your business.

PHILIP: But a man's business is important because that's how he shows he cares.

BETH: Does he? When it makes his family miserable?

PHILIP (*slowly*): Beth, you—you really do hate me, don't you?

BETH: Yes!

LARRY: No, she doesn't, Father. She's just hurt and afraid. None of us hates you. We just don't know you very well.

(*This shocks Philip. Larry is even shocked at himself. Philip walks away from them and stands thinking, with bowed head. They watch silently.*)

PHILIP: I—I see. . . . At least, I'm beginning to see, I think.

(*The phone rings. Larry answers.*)

LARRY: Hello . . . Just a moment. It's for you, Father. Dr. Reeves.

PHILIP (*answering*): Yes, Dr. Reeves . . . Then she will be all right? . . . I see . . . Of course . . . Then there's no use in our coming back? You're sure she won't need one of us tonight? . . . I understand. In the morning, then. Thank you so much for calling . . . Good-bye. (*He hangs up.*)

BETH (*anxiously*): What did he say? Is she all right?

PHILIP (*relieved*): She's resting comfortably and probably won't wake until morning. The X-rays show the head wound.

BETH (*these are the first details for her*): Head wound!

PHILIP: The head wound resulted in a concussion, not a fracture.

LARRY (*to Beth*): She has a fracture though, a broken collar bone. She's all trussed up like a bird ready to fly on one wing.

BETH: Larry!

LARRY: She'll probably say the same thing. You know Mother.

PHILIP: She also has a badly sprained ankle and a gash on her right hand. Plus assorted bruises. The doctor says she'll be all right, though.

BETH: With all that? Oh, Father! (*She begins to cry and goes into her father's arms. This is so unusual, he looks bewildered and pats her back rather ineptly.*)

PHILIP: There, there. No need to cry now. Didn't you hear? She's going to be all right.

BETH (*sobbing*): I—I was s—so afraid!

PHILIP (*distressed*): Don't cry!

LARRY (*calmly*): Let her cry. She's happy.

(*Beth cries louder at this. Philip is bewildered.*)

PHILIP: Happy?

LARRY: Sure. She and Mom always cry when they are happy.

PHILIP: How do you know?

LARRY: Oh, just being around. You can learn a lot about a person just being around.

PHILIP (*with respect*): I am beginning to see that. Larry, I think I have underestimated you.

LARRY: Probably!

(*Beth ceases. Still sniffling she moves away from her father.*)

BETH: I'm sorry, Father.

PHILIP (*surprised at his feelings*): My pleasure . . . I really mean that. It's been a long time since I comforted anyone! (*embarrassed*) I feel like thanking God for your mother.

BETH: I already did.

PHILIP: He won't take it amiss if I do too, will he? That is, if he remembers who I am!

LARRY: He remembers.

BETH: I'm hungry!

PHILIP: So am I. The news of the accident—

BETH: Oh, dear! What happened to your client?

PHILIP: I don't know! I just took off from Carrington's . . . say, I *am* hungry.

LARRY (*ruefully*): Those TV dinners are all dried out by now.

BETH: What about peanut butter and jelly sandwiches?

PHILIP: That sounds delicious!

BETH: I'll go fix some.

(*She leaves. Larry resumes at the tree. Philip watches and then joins him. They work together.*)

PHILIP: You don't think well of me as a father, do you Larry?

LARRY: Let's not talk about that.

PHILIP: Let's do. Some of the things tonight—well, they've set me thinking. Larry, I do love you and Beth. And Susan. She's an unusual woman.

LARRY: I know.

PHILIP: The divorce was her idea.

LARRY: So you say.

PHILIP: I guess I thought there was just one answer: business, success, and money. That's not it, is it?

LARRY: No.

PHILIP: You are a wise—I started to say "boy" but *person* is better. Maybe wiser than your father.

LARRY (*embarrassed*): Aw, Dad!

PHILIP (*touched*): You haven't called me Dad since you were very little. Thank you.

LARRY (*handing him an ornament*): Here's something to hang.

PHILIP: Just the thing. Larry, how does a man make an about-face in his life?

LARRY: I don't know, Dad.

PHILIP: Can a man start all over?

LARRY: I don't know why not. Seems to me you've just got to care enough. Here. You put the star on top.

(*Beth enters with a small crèche.*)

BETH: Look! I remembered the crèche. Where shall we put it?

LARRY: Here (*indicates at foot of the tree*).

PHILIP: A good place.

BETH: We have to have the crèche. That's what Christmas is all about. (*She puts the pieces in place as she talks.*) The sheep here. And the shepherds. The Wise Men go here. Although the Wise Men came later. Did you know, Dad?

PHILIP: Yes.

BETH: Mary and Joseph here. And the manger with the baby. There! The Holy Family. Isn't it lovely?

LARRY: *Love*ly. That's the right word, Dad. *Love.*

PHILIP: It covers everything.

BETH (*stands back and looks*): Our beautiful little tree! Oh, this is the happiest Christmas we've ever had!

(*Silently they look at each other. Philip turns to Beth.*)

LARRY: Beth, I'll bet you forgot the sandwiches for the crèche!

BETH: Oh, no, I didn't! Come out to the kitchen. I even opened a jar of dill pickles!

PHILIP (*with distaste*): Dill Pickles? With peanut butter and jelly?

BETH: Dad, don't knock it till you've tried it.

LARRY: Yeah, Dad. You might find you like that, too!

(*They all leave.*)

3

"Come Let Us Adore Him"

This is a dramatic worship service based on carols in the *Baptist Hymnal* (1975) except for the "Threefold Amen" found in *Baptist Hymnal.* There are several ways to use the music in this dramatic service:

With all singing done by the congregation

With all singing done by a choir

With singing alternately between the congregation and a choir

As here, with congregation and three choirs: children, youth, adults, plus two soloists.

The service calls for a speaking chorus of eight: four males and four females. There is also a suggested optional pantomime group which performs in center stage. This will add greatly to the production. Pantomime uses the whole body to express the message. Don't stop the flow of sound for the pantomime. It occurs simultaneously.

Be creative. Let your organist devise music background to the speaking chorus. You may want to use biblical costumes for all: singers, speakers, pantomimists. Let each person be responsible for his own. See children's literature for examples. For materials, old sheets, bedspreads, and draperies that have been dyed look more authentic than new materials. Certainly if everyone is costumed, you will arrange them casually in the space available, rather than in regimented rows.

The congregation will need printed guides to follow. Notice that the stanza selection carries the story in sequence, omitting those which are out of consequence. The service lasts 35-40 minutes. Once it begins, let nothing interrupt it, no announcements, no hymn numbers. Let it be a true worship experience.

(*Choirs in place. Center stage open. Speaking chorus at a side.*)

CONGREGATION and CHOIRS: "Holy, Holy, Holy," No. 1, all stanzas.

(Ensuing pantomime: a man bearing a scroll enters center, reads to himself.)

SOLO 1 (*male*): In the beginning was the Word, and the Word was with God.

CHORUS: And the Word was God.

SOLO 2 (*male*): I am Alpha and Omega, the beginning and the end, the first and the last.

CHORUS: And he has on his robe and on his thigh written:

SOLO 3 (*female, loudly*): King of kings!

CHORUS: King of kings!

SOLO 4 (*male*): And Lord of lords!

CHORUS: And Lord of lords!

SOLO 5 (*female*): A virgin shall be with child and shall bear a son. They shall call his name Emmanuel, which means, God with us.

CHORUS: Alleluia and amen!

(Pantomime: man with scroll leaves.)

ALL CHOIRS: "Alleluia," No. 422, stanza 1

(Ensuing pantomime: Mary to stage center, followed by Gabriel. Actors move freely, reacting to flow of story.)

SOLO 6 (*male*): The angel Gabriel was sent from God to a village of Galilee named Nazareth.

SOLO 7 (*female*): To a virgin engaged to marry a man named Joseph.

CHORUS: Of the family of David, the king.

SOLO 7: And the girl's name was Mary.

SOLO 6: The angel appeared before her and said, "Hail, highly favored one! The Lord is with you!"

(*Pantomime: Mary cringes in fear.*)

Solo 7: When she saw him, she was confused and frightened.

Solo 6: "Blessed are you among women!"

Solo 7: "What does this mean?"

Solo 6: "Do not be afraid, Mary. You have found favor with God. Soon you will conceive a child. You will give birth to a son. You shall name him Jesus. He shall be great, and shall be called the Son of God. His rule and his kingdom will have no bounds."

(*Mary is no longer afraid, but awed.*)

Solo 7: Then Mary asked the angel, "How can this be? I am yet a virgin maid."

Solo 6: And the angel replied, "The Holy Spirit shall come upon you."

Chorus (*echoing*): "The Holy Spirit shall come upon you."

Solo 6: "The power of God shall overshadow you."

Chorus (*echoing*): "The power of God shall overshadow you."

Solo 6: "Therefore that Holy Child which shall be born to you shall be called the Son of God."

Chorus (*echoing*): "The Son of God."

Solo 6: "For with God nothing shall be impossible!"

Chorus (*echoing*): "Nothing impossible!"

(*Pantomime: Mary sinks to floor before angel, bowing her face in submission.*)

Solo 7: And Mary said: "I am God's servant. Let it be according to his will."

Chorus: And the angel departed from her.

(*Pantomime: Gabriel leaves. Mary rises in exaltation.*)

Solo 7 (*exalted*): "How I praise God! How I rejoice in my Lord!

He chose this lowly handmaid, and now generations shall call me blessed! He that is mighty has dealt with me greatly! Holy is his name!"

(*Pantomime: Mary leaves.*)

CHORUS (*strongly*): Alleluia and amen!

ALL CHOIRS: "Threefold Amen," *Baptist Hymnal*

CHORUS: Now the birth of Jesus Christ happened this way:

SOLO 8 (*female*): His mother, Mary, was engaged to Joseph. Before they were married, she was found with child by the Holy Spirit.

(*Pantomime: Joseph enters, troubled, comes center, sits on floor as if asleep.*)

SOLO 1: Then Joseph her husband, being a stern and upright man,

CHORUS: But not willing to make her a public spectacle,

SOLO 1: Decided to break the engagement quietly.

(*Ensuing Pantomime: Gabriel enters, approaches Joseph.*)

CHORUS: But while he thought about this, the angel of the Lord appeared to him in a dream, saying,

(*Pantomime: Joseph stirs but does not waken.*)

SOLO 2: "Joseph, son of David, don't fear to take Mary as your wife. The child she carries is by the Holy Spirit. She shall bear a son and you shall call him Jesus, for he shall save his people from their sins."

(*Pantomime: Angel leaves and Joseph wakens.*)

CHORUS: Then Joseph awoke. He did as the angel of the Lord had told him. He took Mary for his wife.

(*Pantomime: Joseph leaves.*)

CONGREGATION and ALL CHOIRS: "O Come, All Ye Faithful," No. 81, all stanzas.

(Ensuing Pantomime: Mary and Joseph slowly cross acting area and off.)

SOLO 3: In those days, Caesar Augustus sent out a decree: in all the world a census shall be taken.

CHORUS: This census was taken when Cyrenius was governor of Syria. Everyone went to his ancestral home to be registered.

SOLO 5: So Joseph went up from Galilee out of the village of Nazareth

CHORUS: To the ancestral home of David which is Bethlehem,

SOLO 5: Because Joseph was a member of the family of David.

CHORUS: He took with him Mary, who, by this time, was great with child.

YOUTH CHOIR: "O Little Town of Bethlehem" No. 85, stanzas 1,2.
ADULT CHOIR: "Silent Night, Holy Night" No. 89, stanzas 1,3,4.

(Ensuing Pantomime: Mary, with an imaginary baby cradled in her arms, enters slowly with Joseph. Slowly she places the imaginary child into an imaginary manger at the back of the acting area, covering him carefully. The two look lovingly at the baby. Mary sits on the floor beside the manger, and Joseph takes his place behind them. They freeze in place for the time being.)

CHORUS: And so it was, that while they were there, the time came for the birth of her baby.

SOLO 8: And she bore her firstborn son and wrapped him in swaddling clothes and laid him in a manger in the stable,

CHORUS: Because there was no room for them in the inn.

SOLOIST: "Child in the Manger," No. 84, all 3 stanzas.
CHILDREN'S CHOIR: "Away in a Manger," No. 80, all 3 stanzas.
ADULT CHOIR: "Hark! The Herald Angels Sing," No. 83,

stanzas 1,2.

YOUTH CHOIR: "The First Nowell the Angel Did Say," No. 91, stanzas 1,2.

(Ensuing pantomime: The shepherds enter, go to front of acting area. Gabriel enters. Their terror. At least one will fall to floor, others cower. As angel continues, they lose fear but not awe, especially on hearing all the angels.)

CHORUS: In the nearby fields, shepherds were keeping watch over their flock during the night.

SOLO 8: Suddenly an angel of the Lord appeared before them.

SOLO 4: And the light of the glory of the Lord shone round about them.

CHORUS: And they were terrified.

SOLO 6: But the angel said: "Fear not! I bring you news of great joy!"

CHORUS: "This news is for everybody."

SOLO 6: "For today in the city of David is born the Savior."

CHORUS: "He is Christ the Lord!"

SOLO 6: "You will know it is he, when you shall find the baby wrapped in swaddling clothes and lying in a manger."

CHORUS: And suddenly a multitude of the heavenly host joined the angel, praising God and saying,

SOLOS 1,3 (*strongly*): "Glory to God in the highest!"

SOLOS 2,5 (*strongly, overlapping*): "Glory to God in the highest!"

SOLOS 4,7 (*strongly, overlapping*): "Glory to God in the highest!"

SOLOS 6,8 (*strongly, overlapping*): "Glory to God in the highest!"

CHORUS (*strongly*): "Glory to God in the highest! And on earth peace! Peace, good will toward men! Glory to God!"

(Pantomime: all pantomimists freeze during singing.)

ALL CHOIRS: "It Came Upon the Midnight Clear" No. 86, stanza 1.
CHILDREN'S CHOIR: "Go, Tell It on the Mountain" No. 82, all stanzas.
YOUTH CHOIR: "Glory Be to God on High" No. 104, stanzas 1,4,5.
ADULT CHOIR: "Angels We Have Heard on High" No. 95, stanzas 1,3,4.

(*Ensuing pantomime: the angel leaves. Shepherds confer excitedly, walk around area to manger scene. React to wonder of child. Freeze during next singing.*)

CHORUS: When the angels were gone away from them into heaven, the shepherds said one to another,

SOLO 1: "Let us now go to Bethlehem."

SOLO 2: "Let us see this thing which has happened, which the Lord has told us about."

CHORUS: And they hurried to the village and found Mary and Joseph and the baby lying in a manger.

SOLO: "There's a Song in the Air," No. 93, stanzas 1,4.
ADULT CHOIR: "Infant Holy, Infant Lowly," No. 94, both stanzas.

(*Ensuing pantomime: The shepherds describe the angels to Mary and Joseph. They leave, rejoicing. During the next song, Mary and Joseph leave. Don't forget the baby!*)

CHORUS: And when they had seen, they told everybody what was told them concerning this child.

SOLO 4: And all they who heard the story were amazed at the things which the shepherds told them.

SOLO: But Mary treasured all these things in her heart and thought about them.

CHORUS: Then the shepherds returned to their sheep, glorifying and praising God, for all the things they had heard and seen, just as the angel told them.

Congregation and All Choirs: "Joy to the World! The Lord Is Come," No. 88, stanzas 1,2,4; "Good Christian Men, Rejoice" No. 90, all 3 stanzas.

(*The speaking CHORUS comes to stage center for the remainder.*)

Chorus (*slower tempo*): For unto us a child is born, unto us a son is given:

Solo 7: And the government shall be upon his shoulder.

Solo 1: And his name shall be called *Wonderful!*

Chorus (*swelling and fading*): WON-der-ful.

Solo 8: Counsellor!

Chorus: Counsellor!

Solo 2: The mighty God!

Chorus: The mighty God!

Solo 4: The everlasting Father!

Chorus: The everlasting Father!

Solo 3: The Prince of Peace!

Chorus: The Prince of Peace!

Solo 5: Of the increase of his government and peace

Chorus: There shall be no end.

Solo 6: Upon the throne of David, and upon his kingdom,

Chorus: To order it, and to establish it with judgment and with justice, From henceforth even *for ever!*

Congregation and All Choirs: "How Great Thou Art," No. 35, all 4 stanzas.

4
The Dream

(The three males in this biblical skit may wear contemporary clothing. A scarf wrapped around the head of Joseph and Mary's father, and a white strip of old sheeting draped across the head and shoulders of the Angel, will be costume enough. Three folding chairs side by side can be Joseph's bed. As the skit begins, Mary's father and Joseph are talking.)

FATHER (*sadly*): Joseph, we will not blame you if you break the engagement.

JOSEPH (*hurt and stubborn*): It is my right!

FATHER: Indeed it is. But I must tell you, Mary's mother and I believe her.

JOSEPH: I would like to believe her, but we are human beings and we are as we are. A child is born. It has a mother *and* a father.

FATHER: Joseph, Mary does not lie. Her voice, her face declare she is telling the truth now. She is with child by supernatural means. . . . God, she says.

JOSEPH (*bitterly*): To others, such words are blasphemy!

FATHER: To you?

JOSEPH (*brokenly*): To me? I don't know. As you say, Mary does not lie. If there were a man, wouldn't I know it? And yet, oh, I don't know what to do. Let me sleep on it. I will decide tomorrow.

(Father leaves. Joseph lies down to sleep. In a few moments the angel enters and stands by Joseph's feet. He does not awaken although he stirs restlessly.)

ANGEL (*gently*): Joseph, son of David, do you hear me?

JOSEPH (*eyes closed in sleep*): Yes.

ANGEL: You are troubled.

JOSEPH (*sighs*): Yes.

ANGEL: This problem of Mary worries you?

JOSEPH: Oh, yes!

ANGEL: She is telling the truth. Believe her. You were right. She does not lie.

JOSEPH (*in despair*): Then I don't understand.

ANGEL: Is it necessary for you to understand?

JOSEPH: For my peace of mind! The elders, the town—

ANGEL (*sternly*): Is it better to please men, or Almighty God?

JOSEPH (*doubtfully*): I see. I think I do.

ANGEL: Joseph, the child is there because of the Holy Spirit. Do you understand?

JOSEPH (*doubtfully*): I—I guess so.

ANGEL (*trying another approach*): Do you know I am really here, Joseph?

JOSEPH: I am dreaming. . . . Am I dreaming?

ANGEL: In a way. But you are dreaming truth. Joseph, do not hesitate to take Mary to be your wife. Care for her. When the child is born, he will be a son. Joseph, you are to call him Jesus.

JOSEPH (*surprised*): Jesus? No one in our family has that name. We always name after someone in the family.

ANGEL: The name means Savior. He is to be called Jesus because he will save his people from their sins. Do you understand?

JOSEPH (*after a pause*): I—I think so.

ANGEL: Joseph, you still doubt. Tomorrow go to the Temple.

Read again the prophet Isaiah who declared, "Behold a virgin shall conceive and bear a son and shall call his name Immanuel, God with us." Don't you see, Joseph? Mary is the one chosen of God. It is important that you understand. Do you hear me, Joseph?

JOSEPH: I hear.

ANGEL: Do you understand?

JOSEPH: I understand. But I can't—I am a plain man.

ANGEL (*as he stops*): Yes, Joseph?

JOSEPH (*with emotion*): When I wake and go tell Mary . . . and we are married . . . and the child. . . . Oh, no!

ANGEL: Yes, Joseph? Something troubles you still?

JOSEPH (*deeply moved*): God knows I am only a simple carpenter! If this is as you say, how can *I* ever be father to such a child as *this*?

ANGEL (*smiles tenderly*): You will, Joseph. You will. God chose you, too. Now, sleep. Sleep the sleep you deserve.

(*The angel leaves. In a moment Joseph wakes. Slowly he stands and looks around. Then he lifts his face to heaven with closed eyes as if in prayer. After a moment he leaves purposefully.*)

5
"King of the Jews"

(*The five characters in this biblical background skit may wear biblical costumes; or they may wear ordinary clothing with the addition of appropriate crowns, turbans, sashes, and the like. Staging: one chair center for the king and three at one side for the visitors from the east. Characters are:* Herod, *servant, and the visitors from the east who are sometimes called* Melchior, Balthasar *and* Caspar. *To begin, Herod enters, goes to his chair, talking to his servant.*)

HEROD (*impatient*): Men from the east to see me? Tell them in two or three days.

SERVANT: But your majesty—

HEROD: I can't grant an audience to just anyone who comes to the palace door! I am the king! Let them wait.

SERVANT: Your majesty, these are not ordinary men.

HEROD (*interested*): Oh?

SERVANT: Sire, they have many camels with saddles and trappings of the finest leather and studs of gold. The many guards and servants wear fine clothing. The men themselves have robes of purple with jeweled collars and rings and chains of gold.

HEROD (*thoughtfully*): All that? Then, perhaps I will make an exception. Show them in.

SERVANT: Yes, sire. (*He leaves and returns with the three.*) Sire, your visitors.

HEROD: Welcome, gentlemen, to my palace. I am honored by the visit of so distinguished a company. Please be seated.

(*They bow and sit in chairs to Herod's right.*)

HEROD: Now, how can I help you?

MELCHIOR: We have come to find the king of the Jews.

HEROD: I am king of the Jews.

CASPAR: You don't understand, sire. You see—

BALTHASAR (*interrupting*): We are astrologers. We study the stars and the history and prophecies of the world.

HEROD (*impatiently*): I know what astrologers do!

MELCHIOR: Our stars tell us one is born who is to be king of the Jews.

HEROD (*proudly*): My son will be king after me.

BALTHASAR: Not your son. This child is foretold in the prophecies of the Jews. No, sire, not your son. Another.

HEROD: Impossible!

CASPAR: But, sire, we have seen his star! We have followed it here. He already has been born!

MELCHIOR: You see, we thought you might know where he is. But if not, we will search elsewhere. Forgive our intrusion. (*He starts to rise.*)

HEROD: No, no! Wait! I will consult with my wise men. Meantime, my servants will show you to your quarters. Rest from your journey. You will hear from me soon.

(*The three leave. The servant remains.*)

HEROD: Go to my priests and scribes. Ask about prophecies! I intend to be the only king of the Jews!

(*The servant hurries out. Herod freezes, remaining motionless for a long pause. Then the servant returns.*)

SERVANT: Sire, your religious leaders say the Messiah will be born in Bethlehem, according to the prophet Micah.

HEROD: (*craftily*): Bring the astrologers from the east! There is no time to lose.

(*The servant leaves and returns with the three. They bow before Herod. He pretends eagerness and good will.*)

HEROD: Sires, my wise men have your answer! The prophecy says the Messiah will be born in Bethlehem. This is a small village about three days' journey. I am sure you will want to continue on your way immediately. I understand this desire. It is mine also. But duty keeps me here. Oh, that I might see the Messiah at last!

MELCHIOR: We will leave in the morning.

CASPAR: We will continue to follow our star.

BALTHASAR: If it does not lead to Bethlehem, we will follow wherever it leads.

HEROD: When you have found him, come back this way. I shall wait eagerly for news. I want to see him and worship him, too!

MELCHIOR (*bowing*): As you say, your majesty.

(They all bow and leave, led by the servant. In a moment, Herod rises, turns his back to the audience and freezes. A lengthy pause, then the servant hurries in, excited. Herod turns.)

SERVANT: Your majesty! News!

HEROD: What news?

SERVANT: The men from the east! They have gone by another route!

HEROD (*angrily*): Take soldiers! Go after them at once!

SERVANT (*nervously*): It is too late, sire. Bedouins in the desert saw them many days ago. Your soldiers could never catch them!

HEROD (*pacing, enraged*): They crossed me! Where *is* this child?

SERVANT: Somewhere in Bethlehem, sire.

HEROD: Why has no one come from Bethlehem to tell *me* he has been born? Why?

SERVANT: I know not, sire.

HEROD: They fear me! That's why! Well, *I* am king of the Jews and my son after me! This child is just another child. You understand?

SERVANT: Yes, sire.

HEROD (*enraged*): But he could cause trouble! These Jews are superstitious. They might raise him up a following. Then what would happen?

SERVANT: I know not.

HEROD (*incensed*): Of course you don't! You are stupid! But I know! Those cursed Romans long for an excuse to make things difficult for me. That's what would happen! Do you see?

SERVANT: Yes, sire.

HEROD (*still pacing*): Well, I won't have it! Do you hear? I will find this child, and he shall die!

SERVANT: How will you find him, sire?

HEROD (*stands still, thinking; then, deliberately*): I will find him because I will kill every baby boy under two years of age in Bethlehem!

SERVANT (*horrified*): You—you wouldn't!

HEROD: Why not? I would kill a man who came at me with a knife.

SERVANT (*appalled*): But—babies?

HEROD: It's the same. Call my captains! They shall take my soldiers and destroy that which would destroy me. All the boy children in Bethlehem. Go, quickly! (*The servant hurries out.*) Somewhere among those children *he* will be! Then we shall see who will be king of the Jews!

(*Herod leaves, still angry.*)

6

Gabriel, Blow!

(*The cast of this imaginary, satirical skit is three angels and a* deep voice *off stage. Not all angels were perfect. See* 2 *Peter* 2:4. Gabriel *is a male.* Probus *and* Aptus *are male names. If females play these parts, rename them Proba and Apta. Dress in costumes if available. If not, with ordinary clothing, wear long white scarves draped across their heads and shoulders. Strips of soft old sheets will do. As the skit begins, angels Probus and Aptus enter one side of the playing area.*)

APTUS: (*peevishly*): Oh, my! Here comes Gabriel again!

PROBUS (*quickly*): Pretend we don't see him! (*They turn their backs.*)

(*Angel Gabriel enters from the other side, sees the two.*)

GABRIEL (*pompously*): Oh, there you are! I was looking for you. I am leaving again.

APTUS (*still with back turned*): Good-bye.

GABRIEL (*patronizing*): Naturally you want to know where I'm going.

PROBUS (*faces him*): Not particularly.

GABRIEL (*persisting*): I know you've heard about the special missions I've been on.

APTUS (*turning*): We've heard.

GABRIEL: Yes. Well, this mission is tied in with the others.

APTUS: That's nice.

GABRIEL: They were all very important. So don't you think it strange he's let me take my horn only once?

PROBUS: We haven't thought about it.

GABRIEL: Well, think about it! Remember the first of this series of missions?

APTUS: If I say no, you'll tell us; and if I say yes, you'll tell us anyway.

GABRIEL: Forging right ahead, the first one was to a priest named Zacharias. As a result, he and his wife had a son.

PROBUS: So you told us before.

APTUS: And told us.

GABRIEL: Oh? Did I tell you the next mission was to that young girl, Mary? About *the baby*.

APTUS (*affectedly*): Probus, I think Gabriel told us. Don't you think he told us?

PROBUS: I do declare I believe he did tell us!

GABRIEL (*ignoring their manner*): Good. She was a nice young thing. I suppose my horn would have been out of place there.

APTUS: Unless you wanted to scare her to death.

GABRIEL: Next I had to straighten out the thinking of her husband-to-be. Joseph was his name.

PROBUS: So you said.

APTUS: You sure did!

GABRIEL (*blandly*): I did? Then you know I was sent to those shepherds outside Bethlehem?

APTUS (*gleefully*): Yes! But he sent a bunch with you that time!

GABRIEL: Only for the chorus effect! *I* was in charge! *I* made the main announcement! *And* I played my horn!

APTUS: Bully for you!

PROBUS: We concede.

GABRIEL: I should think so!

PROBUS: Have a nice journey.

APTUS: Bye, bye, Gabriel!

(*They turn to go but Gabriel stops them.*)

GABRIEL: Wait! I haven't told you all of it!

PROBUS: I'm sure you have.

APTUS: More than once, wouldn't you say, Probus?

PROBUS: Oh, definitely.

GABRIEL: Nevertheless, to understand this new mission, you have to hear it all.

PROBUS: All right. But make it fast.

GABRIEL: Some things are not to be hurried. Now, the next

mission in this series was when I told some astrologers who went to see that baby—I told them to go home another way.

PROBUS and APTUS: And avoid Jerusalem!

APTUS: Yes, we know.

GABRIEL (*annoyed*): Oh, very well. Did I tell you I didn't use my horn then?

PROBUS: No, but since those astrologers were trying to avoid attention, I'm sure they were grateful.

GABRIEL: Oh? Well, perhaps. At any rate, I have a mission *today*.

PROBUS: That's nice. Isn't it nice, Aptus?

APTUS: Indeed it is, Probus. Nice.

GABRIEL: You want to know where?

APTUS: Never mind.

GABRIEL: It's no bother. I'm going back to Joseph. He's the one who married that young girl who—

PROBUS: We know!

GABRIEL: Well, *He* wants to get them out of Judea and into Egypt. That family, I mean. Want to know why?

PROBUS: He always has his reasons.

GABRIEL: Yes. Well, Herod—he's a king around there—Herod is going to have all children under two killed.

APTUS (*shocked*): All of them?

GABRIEL: That's right.

APTUS: Isn't that rather—wasteful?

GABRIEL: Herod doesn't care. So He wants the family out. I'm going to tell them to leave.

APTUS: Have a nice trip.

GABRIEL: Did you ever wonder why neither of you is ever sent on a mission?

PROBUS: Not much.

GABRIEL (*proudly*): *He* picks the most intelligent, the most dependable angels for these important missions!

APTUS: Well, we're both busy in the angelic choir anyway. You've got to have *talent* for that.

GABRIEL: Have you heard me play my horn?

PROBUS: Noisy, isn't it?

GABRIEL: Are you jealous of all my accomplishments and honors? . . . That's it! You're jealous!

DEEP VOICE: Aptus! Probus!

APTUS and PROBUS (*looking around nervously*): Y—yes, Lord?

DEEP VOICE: Gabriel is right. You are jealous. Don't you know envy is a sin?

APTUS and PROBUS: Y—yes, Lord.

DEEP VOICE: When you are ready in spirit, I will send you on important missions.

APTUS and PROBUS (*meekly*): Y—yes, Lord.

GABRIEL: What did I tell you?

DEEP VOICE: Gabriel!

GABRIEL (*calmly*): Yes, Lord?

DEEP VOICE: Gabriel, this is your last mission.

GABRIEL (*bewildered*): *Last* mission? But I've done so well! Everybody knows it. (*to others*) Don't you?

PROBUS: So you told us.

APTUS: And told us.

GABRIEL (*rebelliously*): Why is it my last mission when I'm doing so well?

DEEP VOICE: You are filled with pride. I will send another messenger after this.

GABRIEL: It isn't fair!

DEEP VOICE: Gabriel!

GABRIEL (*meekly*): As you say, Lord. Well at least I have my special mission at THE END.

DEEP VOICE: Better forget that mission.

GABRIEL (*pleading*): But you *have* to let me! (*with a touch of egotism*) What will you do then without my *horn*?

DEEP VOICE: Oh, I'll think of something.

7

Will the Real Santa Claus Please Stand Up?

(*The three characters in this contemporary skit are* Mother; Lisa, *her teenaged daughter; and* Billie, *an eight-year-old, can be either a boy or girl. Mother sits mending or knitting when Billie enters.*)

BILLIE: Mom, why didn't you tell me a long time ago there wasn't any Santa Claus?

MOTHER: Billie, you are only eight now. It's nice for little children to believe in Santa. Remember what fun it was to write your letter to him each year?

BILLIE: I guess.

MOTHER (*teasing*): Besides, most children behave so well just before Christmas! It's a pleasure for their parents.

BILLIE: Aw, Mom!

MOTHER: Then, too, if you hadn't believed in Santa, why hang up your sock? Think of missing the thrill of that filled sock on Christmas morning.

BILLIE: Yeah. I got some neat things in my sock, didn't I?

MOTHER: Yes, you did. I'm just sorry you had to find out. Think of all that fun lasting at least another year.

BILLIE: Aw, Mom! I'm not a little kid any more!

(*Lisa enters.*)

LISA: Hi, family! What's to eat?

MOTHER: Your father wants early supper—5:30. There's a deacon's meeting. So don't spoil your appetite with snacks. Eat an apple.

LISA: Oh, I'll wait. (*Sits and sighs.*) Boy, what a day! I bet our drill team marched forty 'leven miles after school.

BILLIE (*importantly*): Lisa—

LISA: Yeah?

BILLIE: Lisa, I have to tell you something you ought to know.

LISA: Fire away, shrimp.

BILLIE (*confiding*): Lisa, there really isn't any Santa Claus. You ought to know that.

LISA: Well, thanks! Mom?

MOTHER: Billie found out today.

LISA: Billie, I'm sorry!

BILLIE: I guess you have to know things.

LISA: Yes, but—well, I was sorry afterward that I knew. At least so soon. It was fun while it lasted.

BILLIE (*sadly*): Yeah. (*perks up*) Judy and Steve don't know yet!

LISA: Don't tell them. Don't tell any of your friends.

BILLIE: What if I just say I know something they don't know?

MOTHER: Not even that. They'd pester you into telling.

BILLIE: If they start to talk about Santa—

LISA: Billie, don't you dare say a word! Don't even snicker!

BILLIE (*rebelliously*): What do I do? Just stand there holding my mouth shut?

LISA: Not a bad idea.

MOTHER: Now, Billie, I expect to be obeyed.

BILLIE: But, Mom—

MOTHER: No buts. If I find out you have told anyone, or even let slip one word—I don't like to make threats, but I am serious about this.

BILLIE (*grudgingly*): Okayyyy.

MOTHER: That's good.

BILLIE: If there's no Santa, when I hang up my sock—

LISA: What's the point? No more socks with Christmas goodies for you! I see where Mom and Dad save some money.

BILLIE: No sock at all? That's gross! If you have to give up Santa anyway, what's the point in ever believing? Who thought it up, anyway?

MOTHER: I don't know. Someone who loved children. Someone who wanted to give them pleasure out of that love.

BILLIE (*after thinking for a long pause*): I guess Santa Claus must be like Jesus.

MOTHER: Oh, no, Billie!

LISA: Wait, Mom. Why not? The Bible says God is love. Jesus was born because God loved us. Maybe Santa is just another way of showing love—a human way.

MOTHER: Well, maybe.

LISA: So Billie is right. Santa is like Jesus.

MOTHER (*protesting*): Lisa, you'll give Billie a wrong idea.

BILLIE: No, she won't. I get it.

LISA: See? Billie is as bright as I am.

BILLIE: What's really like Jesus is your Dad. And your Mom. They are the ones who love you.

MOTHER: Maybe Billie is brighter than you are, Lisa!

LISA: Oh, *Mom!*

8
Unto One of These

(*This skit has two boys around thirteen years old,* Bobby *and* Joey, Bobby's mother, *and an off-stage* Voice. *At one side of the playing area sits Mother reading a Bible. On the other side of the playing area stand Bobby and Joey. Mother freezes.*)

BOBBY: Day after tomorrow it's Christmas and a whole week before we go back to school. There's time. Joey, if you can't get the money for the sweater from your Mom, why don't you earn it?

JOEY: No one will hire you when you're only thirteen. I tried every place anyone suggested. I *could* get a job delivering papers if I had a bicycle. Mr. Perkins said so. My Mom can't afford one. I guess I'll have to get out of the boys' chorus.

BOBBY: I think I'm getting a new bike for Christmas. A ten-speed.

JOEY (*glad for him*): That's great!

BOBBY: Mom and Dad don't know I know! What are you getting?

JOEY: A new pair of shoes.

BOBBY: *Shoes?* Shoes are something you buy because you need them.

JOEY: Not at my house. Well, so long, Bobby. Merry Christmas!

BOBBY: So long, Joey, and the same to you, if I don't see you.

(*Joey freezes in place. Bobby goes to his mother.*)

BOBBY (*troubled*): Mom, are you busy?

MOTHER: Just going over the Bible lesson again. How is Joey?

BOBBY: Okay.

MOTHER: Joey is a good friend, isn't he?

BOBBY: Yeah. Mom, are we rich?

MOTHER (*laughs*): No, indeed!

BOBBY (*anxiously*): Are we poor?

MOTHER: No, not that either. We're somewhere in between.

BOBBY: What is being poor?

MOTHER: Well, there's *destitute,* which means you have nothing. Poor means you don't have enough money to buy what you need.

BOBBY (*thoughtfully*): If your mother doesn't have the money to buy you a sweater, or if she can't buy you a bike—especially if you could get a job delivering papers if you had one—and if you have to call the shoes you need your Christmas present, is that poor?

MOTHER: It could be, Son. That's a lot of ifs. Is it about Joey? I know his mother works very hard.

BOBBY: Well, Joey's dad is dead and his mom works at Pierce's.

MOTHER: I know.

BOBBY: You know those sweaters the kids are buying?

MOTHER: For the boys' chorus?

BOBBY: Yes. Well, Joey's mom can't afford to buy him one. I guess she doesn't make enough money. Joey's thinking of getting out of the chorus.

MOTHER: That would be too bad. Joey has a good voice.

BOBBY: Yeah. Well, if he had a bicycle, he could deliver papers and earn the money. Mr. Perkins said so.

MOTHER: That would be good.

BOBBY: But his mother can't buy him one.

MOTHER: I'm so sorry.

BOBBY: You know what, Mom?

MOTHER: What?

BOBBY: Joey's my best friend. He's a good guy.

MOTHER: I think so, too.

BOBBY: If I gave him my bicycle—

MOTHER: Then what would you do?

BOBBY (*embarrassed*): The truth is—I heard you and Dad talking. You are getting me a new ten-speed, aren't you?

MOTHER: Oh, Bobby, we didn't want you to guess! Your Dad wanted to surprise you.

BOBBY: I didn't mean to hear! Honest, Mom! It just happened. Is it that one from Copley's?

MOTHER (*sighs*): Yes. The one you wanted.

BOBBY: Oh, boy!

MOTHER: It is a beautiful bike. Your Dad brought it home yesterday and hid it upstairs.

BOBBY: Then can I give my old bike to Joey? Please Mom!

MOTHER: We should speak to your Dad first. But he probably will say yes.

BOBBY: Thanks, Mom! You and Dad are swell! I'll go tell Joey!

(*Mother freezes again. Bobby goes to Joey.*)

BOBBY: Joey, guess what! I've got a bicycle for you so you can take that job with the paper!

JOEY (*elated*): Really? Where did you get it?

BOBBY: It's my bicycle. I was right—my folks have a ten-speed for me!

JOEY: That's great!

BOBBY: So you can have my old one.

JOEY: Thanks a lot, Bobby! Oh, boy! Now I can get the job. And the sweater. And even help my Mom out.

BOBBY: Yeah!

JOEY: I was feeling pretty low. I like the chorus.

BOBBY: We have fun.

JOEY: Thanks a whole lot!

BOBBY: Aw, that's okay. Now let me tell you some things you need to know about that bike. The seat wobbles. But don't worry. It won't come off. At least it never has.

JOEY: That's okay. I'll fix it.

BOBBY: The left pedal drags sometimes. When it does, just kick it hard.

JOEY: I will.

BOBBY: The back tire is getting thin. Don't go over glass or sharp rocks.

JOEY: I won't.

BOBBY: Where the front wheel fastens on? You know those screws?

JOEY: I—I guess.

BOBBY: Well, I'll show you. You have to twist them once in a while or the frame comes apart.

JOEY: Okay. I'll twist them. (*Bobby says nothing. After a pause, Joey continues*) Is that all? (*Bobby is still silent.*) Is something wrong?

BOBBY (*slowly*): Just thinking. . . . Just thinking about that bike.

JOEY (*quickly*): If you don't want to give it up, that's okay! I know you like that old bike.

BOBBY: It has lots of things wrong with it. Maybe it wouldn't hold up to delivering papers every day. At least not for long.

JOEY: I'd take good care of it!

BOBBY (*slowly*): Joey, I—I've changed my mind.

JOEY (*trying to hide his disappointment*): That's okay, Bobby! It's your bike.

BOBBY: You know what? I'm going to give you my *new* bike!

JOEY: Huh?

BOBBY: My new bike! You can have my new bike!

JOEY (*laughs nervously*): You're joking! Huh, Bobby?

BOBBY: No, I'm not.

JOEY (*unbelieving*): Aw, Bobby, you know your folks won't let you give a new bike away!

BOBBY: My Mom and Dad—I think they will.

JOEY: Golly!

BOBBY: Besides, my old bike—well, I understand it better than anyone. I'm going home right now and get my new bike for you!

JOEY (*dazed*): Even if—if they say no—well, thanks anyway!

(*Joey freezes. Bobby returns to his mother.*)

MOTHER: Was Joey surprised?

BOBBY: Mom, you wouldn't believe it!

(*They both freeze.*)

VOICE OFFSTAGE: Ye have done it unto one of the least of these!

(*Actors leave.*)

9

We Didn't Forget Anyone

(The ten characters in this skit all dress similarly, at least in color. At the back of the playing area, place a two-step riser, either portable steps or a tall box or platform with a shorter box or platform in front. As the skit begins, five enter from one side and five from the other and line up across the back on either side of the steps with their faces to the wall. See Figure 1. Select speakers by height: 10, 5,9,4,8,3,7,2,6,1. In the skit when they move, they will realign as in Figure 2.)

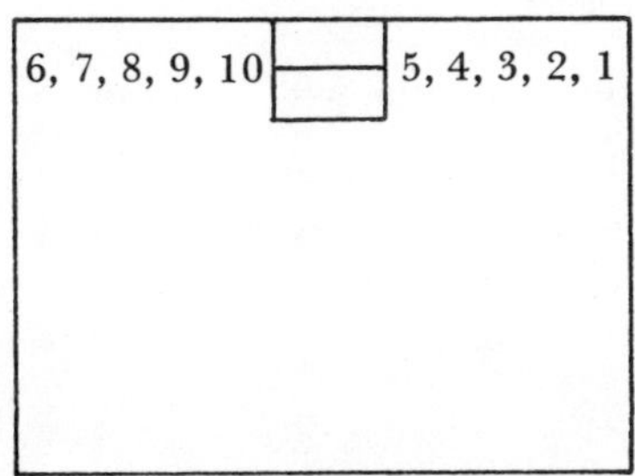

Figure 1

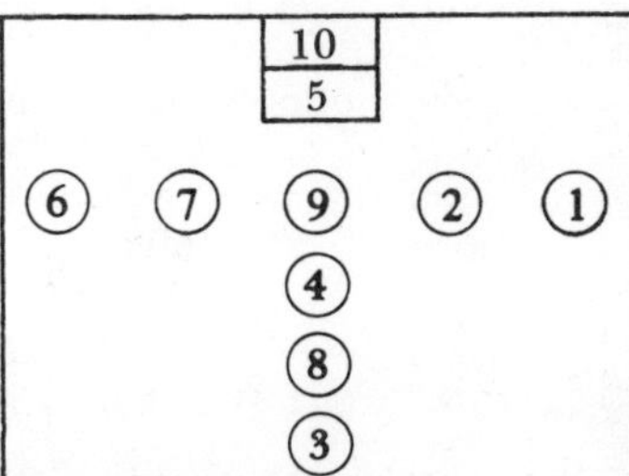

Figure 2

No. 1 (*turns to audience*): That is really a beautiful tree!

No. 2 (*turns*): I think so. Of course the man overcharged me dreadfully. But I *had* to have this one. The branches are so full and symmetrical.

No. 3 (*playfully*): Let's all congratulate ourselves on the super way we decorated it.

No. 4 (*turns*): Speaking of money, let's be careful when we take it all down. Those baubles cost plenty.

No. 5 (*turns*): Why didn't you use the old ones?

No. 4: Some of those *are* the old ones. But they weren't nearly enough.

No. 2: This tree is bigger than last year's, isn't it?

No. 4: Yes. That's why I had to buy more decoration. You'd think those things were made of gold, the way they cost.

No. 6 (*turns*): Don't mention gold. See that little box under the tree? The green one with the Santa Claus on top? Well, that's the gold pin for Isabelle. It's a little package, but I paid enough for it to buy myself a complete outfit!

No. 3: Then why did you get it?

No. 6: Oh, she's been wanting it, and Christmas is the time you always spend more than you have!

No. 7 (*turns*): That doll for Sally Ann? I spent twenty-five dollars for that doll!

No. 5: Sally Ann is too old for dolls.

No. 7: She collects them now, didn't you know? This one is special.

No. 8 (*turns*): My folks and I have a surefire way to enjoy spending at Christmas.

No. 9 (*turns*): How's that?

No. 10 (*turns*): Yes, we'd all like to know.

No. 8: Oh, we just charge everything and the bills don't come due until February 1.

No. 9: Then what do you do on February 1?

No. 8 (*laughs*): Wonder why we were so stupid!

No. 10: Well, we are sensible about Christmas. We buy all year during sales. One gift after another. By the time Christmas comes, we have them all.

No. 1: What's the advantage of that?

No. 10: For one thing, spaced out like that, we can buy much more expensive gifts for everybody.

No. 9: Doesn't that take all the fun out of it? That last minute frantic scramble is part of Christmas!

No. 2: And the kinfolks all coming for dinner. How's the turkey coming?

No. 1: From the way it smells—wonderful!

No. 3: Having three kinds of pie is a good idea. I like cherry, Aunt Flo likes mincemeat, and Robert's favorite is apple.

No. 4: No pecan pie? Who arranged about the pies? It's not Christmas without pecan pie!

No. 6: Greta arranged the pies. Talk to her. Marilyn did the salad.

No. 5: Marilyn did the *tossed* salad. *I* did the fruit salad!

No. 10: You did? Since when is that one of your talents?

No. 5: Don't sneer until you've tasted it.

No. 9: Look at all those presents under that tree! Why, the wrappings alone must have cost—

No. 8: Shhh! Let's not think of it. Or you'll keep the wrappings and throw your gift away.

No. 7: It's too bad they have to be torn off and discarded.

No. 10 (*moves to the top step*): Well, in one of those packages is a watch for Arthur, a *digital* watch I'll finish paying for in April!

No. 5 (*moves to bottom step*): I did the same thing. Mother has a real surprise coming. I can hardly wait to see her face. Now, if I can borrow a ten from her to last the week—

No. 9 (*interrupting, moves to floor below them*): Christmas is for little kids more than the rest of us.

No. 4 (*moving in front of No. 9*): I think so, too. The two of us went together and got that whole train set Bobby has been asking for.

No. 8 (*moving in front of No. 4*): It probably took both of you to pay for it. I heard that set is expensive. Well now, I spent all mine on everyone. Some pretty nice things if I do say so.

No. 3 (*moves in front of No. 8*): So that's why you tried to borrow ten from me? Don't worry, old chum! I sympathize. I did the same thing.

No. 7 (*stands to the right of No. 9*): All of you know how I feel about Carrie and Bill. So don't be surprised when you see their gift from me. The rest of you will have to do with less until next year.

No. 2 (*stands to the left of No. 9*): It's so hard to choose gifts. I must be scatterbrained or something. Every year I resolve to be fair to all. Then I spend more on the first gifts, and, Patty and Jim and Ruth and Frank are the lucky ones this year! The rest of you get gifts that are just so-so.

No. 6 (*stands to the right of No. 7*): Well, I'm not telling what I bought. All I'll say is, don't anybody have a birthday between now and June!

No. 1 (*stands to left of No. 2*): Me, too! I will say this: this is going to be the best Christmas of all. Everybody will get lots of loot. You know, I don't think any of us at all will come out on the short end! We didn't forget anyone!

(*Now, without a sound, 2 and 1, 7 and 6 face toward 9. 4 kneels. 8 sits on the floor. 3 also sits and leans forward, head down, arms extended in front. When 3 extends the arms, all the others do the same, touching the person in front of him. This makes the cross, visible to viewers even in a flat room. Hold for eight actual seconds, then all stand and leave the way they came.*)

10
The Coat

(*Discussion after a drama is profitable. This skit is written especially for small group discussion afterward. In groups of four and five, use the discussion guide at the end. Stage simple: four female characters on stools or levels scattered around the playing area so that none face each other. Each stays in place throughout. When a character is not in the action, she freezes. To begin,* Joanie *and* Mother *are frozen,* Lynn *and* Mindy *speak.*)

LYNN (*eagerly*): Mindy, let's go by Stelke's on our way home.

MINDY (*complaining*): Again? We've been by there every day this week.

LYNN (*willfully*): I don't care! I have to look. If anyone buys that coat—

MINDY: You're cracked about that coat!

LYNN (*intensely*): If I can't have it, I'll just die!

MINDY: Lynn, that coat is too expensive. No one is going to buy it. It will stay right there.

(*Mindy freezes. Mother speaks with Lynn.*)

M*other*: How was school today, Lynn?

LYNN: Okay, I guess. Mother, I went by Stelke's again. Nobody has bought the coat yet.

MOTHER: Lynn, *please* forget about that coat.

LYNN: I can't, Mother! It's so soft. You never saw leather so soft. Like velvet. And it's such a beautiful brown.

MOTHER (*distressed*): I know it's beautiful, dear; but we really can't afford it. Your old coat will have to do for another year.

LYNN (*pleading*): It's so tacky! Christmas is coming, Mom. What about for Christmas?

MOTHER (*regretfully*): Not even for Christmas. Joanie's teeth need straightening and we're saving toward that.

LYNN: Joanie's waited ten years with her same old teeth! She could wait one more!

MOTHER: Lynn, you don't mean that. Besides there are other

things. Your father needs another suit and his overcoat is eight years old.

LYNN (*lightly*): Oh, Dad looks okay in anything. He's a pretty good looking guy.

MOTHER (*patiently*): Also this is the year the house should be painted and the insurance will be due for the next three years.

LYNN (*almost in tears*): You just bring these things up so I won't want the coat, but I do just the same! If I can't have the coat for Christmas, don't buy me anything!

(*Mother freezes. Lynn and Mindy speak.*)

MINDY (*surprised*): Really? You're really getting the coat?

LYNN: Isn't it super?

MINDY: I thought your mother said they couldn't afford it.

LYNN: Oh, she always talks poor. I'm getting it for Christmas. This will be the most wonderful Christmas in the world!

(*Mindy and Lynn freeze. Mother and Joanie speak.*)

JOANIE (*wailing*): Mom! I'll be so old before I'm through wearing braces! I'd almost as soon have these old crooked teeth!

MOTHER: I'm sorry, Joanie. It won't be so bad.

JOANIE: It's that stupid coat, isn't it? Lynn is begging for that stupid coat! It's not fair!

MOTHER: I hate it your father has to wear his old suit and overcoat to the Chicago conference. James is such a fine looking man. He deserves a new outfit for that meeting.

JOANIE: Yeah, he ought to think more of how he dresses.

MOTHER: Oh, he thinks about it; but there's the house insurance. And the house does need painting.

JOANIE: Then don't paint it and let Dad get his clothes.

MOTHER: We've put off painting for another year. This inflation—

JOANIE: You mean with that coat! Mom, why did you let Lynn talk you into it?

(*Mother and Joanie freeze. Pause for eight literal seconds. Then Mindy and Lynn speak.*)

MINDY (*dismayed*): Your coat! There's a big tear in the back.

LYNN (*calmly*): Yeah, I know. A nail in the wall by the stairwell.

MINDY (*sympathetically*): Aren't you just *sick?* Your beautiful coat! Just last Christmas you said you'd die if you couldn't have that coat.

LYNN: Oh, well, I've worn it one season already. It was a little small to begin with. Joanie can mend it and wear it. She won't mind. She's getting her braces Monday.

MINDY: Then what will you wear?

LYNN (*eagerly*): Let's go by Stelke's. I hear they have some dreamy new things in, and Christmas is coming up again soon!

Discussion Guide

1. Do you like these characters? Why?
2. Is the mother a wise mother?
3. What about the unseen father?
4. Are you like Lynn?
5. How would you rate this family as a family?
6. What would you say the skit really was about?

11
The Innkeeper's Wife

I didn't want them to stay. I told my husband, "Send them away." He said: "But she is young and so tired. There is no other inn. Look at her!"

I said, "Oh, I see, all right. What's she doing so far from Galilee in her condition? Where would you put them? In our room?" Then when I saw the consent in his face, I said: "No! Not our room! I am tired and deserve my own bed. You'll have to find somewhere else!"

That didn't change his purpose, and he put them in the stable. Oh, it was clean enough. Every corner of the inn had been burnished for the guests we'd have during the census. So the stable was clean enough with the fresh, sweet smell of new hay and the warm breath of the animals.

I just didn't want them to stay. There they were, tired and dusty from the road and so grateful for a place to rest. The quiet, earnest man, so tender toward his weary young wife. She, with her gentle manner, assenting to his arrangements. And both so poor. The inferior little beast that carried their few possessions, the poor quality of their worn garments, the rudely made sandals on their feet. I fingered my own tunic. Tightly woven threads, the good finish, the evenness of the dye. My sandals were soft and finely sewn, my scarf of sheer linen. How fortunate to have so rich a husband, to live so well each day.

I didn't want them to stay. Not even in the stable. I wanted them to go and never to see them again. Perhaps they would be able to leave in a day or so. Then they would be gone.

But it happened otherwise. In the night, sleeping in my warm bed, I was awakened. My husband said: "Her time is come. Stay with her while I fetch the midwife!" No, I thought, Let someone else stay. But I went. It was a while before the midwife could come. Another life was beginning in Bethlehem that night. So

I stayed. And comforted the girl in this great adventure women share. When the midwife came, I returned to my own bed. Not to sleep. No, not to sleep. Instead to remember. To feel once again the soft little body cradled in my arms, see the rose-petal skin and the tiny hands. My son. My little son whose brief life lasted only long enough to leave an emptiness in my soul.

I didn't want them to stay. Her son (the child was a boy my husband said)—her son sounded healthy enough. "A strong voice!" my husband said, as if he had made that possible. "Being born in a stable may insure a long healthy life!" he said. I didn't see the child. Soon they moved from the stable into a small house elsewhere. Later I heard they left Bethlehem. I didn't see them.

I didn't want them to stay in the first place. Why should I see her son, who probably would live a long, healthy life, and one day would let her hold her grandchildren on her knee, while I—while I had only a memory to hold to my heart? I didn't want them to stay.

12
Mary's Neighbor

Of course I remember Jesus. It's too bad, isn't it? Wasn't I neighbor to his mother when we were girls growing up? Didn't I live in the same town with her after she married Joseph? Just in time, too. But I think we should let bygones be bygones. After all, it was so long ago. At the time, though, well, you know how narrow small towns can be. Remember, the law was the law. If it had been anyone else but Joseph. You didn't know Joseph? Now there was a good man. A saint if ever there was one.

When he became engaged to Mary, everyone thought what a fortunate girl. Oh, she was pretty enough and seemed a modest, sensible girl. Then suddenly there she was—pregnant! Nobody had even a hint of who the man might be. Joseph? Oh, no! No one ever treated a girl with more respect than Joseph. No one gave him a second guess. But then, no one else was likely either. That story she told, about the vision of an angel and God being the father of the child. Well, just let one of *my* daughters or granddaughters try that on *me!*

We expected Joseph to call off the engagement. He had a right if ever a man did. In a few days, though, he married her. Everyone was surprised, to say the least.

We didn't want to offend Joseph, but the whole thing was a little irregular, and so they were left alone. Then they went off to Bethlehem when that census was taken. She didn't have any business going, as far along as she was. But she went. It didn't surprise me to hear the baby had come. It was a while before they returned. Abner, the tentmaker, came back from Bethlehem with that fanciful story. You haven't heard it? I thought everyone had by this time. No, I don't mind telling it. The story goes that some shepherds tending flocks near Bethlehem saw an angel that told them the Messiah was born in Bethlehem. According to the story, that was Jesus. Yes, Mary's baby. Remember Mary said she saw an angel, too. How do I know if it was the same angel? Or if there ever was an angel in the first place. All I know is, *I* never saw an angel and none of my family ever saw an angel and I'd stack my children against Mary's any day!

Well, yes, there were more children besides Jesus. Six or seven anyway. James, the one next to Jesus, and Jude, one of the younger boys, got into that movement Jesus started. It was after Jesus died though.

Going back to the story, when Mary and Joseph finally came back here, Jesus wasn't a baby any longer. He did grow into a fine lad. No, I don't know if he ever saw any angels, but he sure could have used one in Jerusalem that day. You just never know about children. It's a good thing Mary couldn't see into the future when she first held Jesus in her arms. I guess it's a blessing none of us can see what's ahead.

13

The Wise Men

For a time, I thought that prophet from Nazareth might be the baby we saw in Bethlehem long ago. But I could remember seeing nothing in the stars to predict so terrible an end. The stars—well, my fellow astrologers and I knew for years there would be this child, for the stars told us so. We searched the heavens and studied our charts. Yes, we agreed, they pointed to one who would be born the King of the Jews. Perhaps in our lifetime.

Then the new star appeared. This had to be the sign! We said we must go find the child and pay homage to him. Few astrologers have been so fortunate as we. So we set out from Persia to travel to Judea. Of course there were Romans everywhere. But the size of our party and the gold we carried paved our way, No one stopped us. After all we were men of influence, and Rome wanted peace on her eastern borders.

I was in my mid-forties, so I endured the arduous journey quite well. However, my companions were much older. They welcomed the sight of Jerusalem and an opportunity to rest. Our star still stood overhead. We sent messengers to the local king, a nominal office under Roman rule. He granted us an audience for a certain day.

We left our rented quarters and made our way to his palace. It was our first sight of this Herod. I distrusted him immediately, but my companions were kinder. His coarse looks revealed his dissolute life, for we heard he followed the Roman style of living rather than the austere way of the Jews. Certainly his people hated him. Our servants heard this in the city and reported to us.

When we told him we were seeking one born King of the Jews, we could see he was shocked, and a little frightened. He promised to look into the matter, and we went to our quarters. Several days passed. Through our servants, we heard of the agitation at the palace. This Herod called in his astrologers and his historians and even the priests of the Temple. Now this Temple was the religious center of the country. The priests confirmed that prophecy said such a king would appear in a small town about ninety miles away, called Bethlehem.

Then Herod sent for us. He assured us of his own anxiety to find this child. If we found him, we must return to tell Herod and to receive his gratitude and honors. So our journey continued to Bethlehem. We made inquiries in the village and listened to tales of miraculous visions occurring when a certain child was born. The villagers pointed to the house where the parents and child were living.

There we found a healthy baby boy, his young mother, and the father who tried to shield him from further publicity. It is not usual for a child to be born in a stable, with rumors of visions, and then later to have that child sought out by a whole retinue from Persia!

We tried to ease the concern of the father by presenting gifts. Although his earnings as a cabinetmaker must have been small, our gifts did not impress him so much as he worried about the mother and child.

We had no doubt this was the child we sought. All our calculations came to this rented house and these very ordinary people. I say ordinary. And yet—

Well, we started back on our journey home. We did not go by way of Jerusalem. I persuaded my companions Herod was not to be trusted. Perhaps my insistence was based on a dream, a vivid dream, which seemed to tell me not to return to Jerusalem. Or maybe my own dislike for the man—at any rate, we returned to Persia by another route.

The years went by. My companions succumbed to old age and only I was left to wonder about this new prophet in Judea—but not for long. This one who died so shamefully could not be that babe of Bethlehem. No, no. I shall continue to wait for news. For did not our stars tell us the one we sought would be king and that his kingdom would never end?

14
The Young Shepherd

(This monologue may be given in shepherd's costume or in modern clothing with a shepherd's headdress. A monologue is not merely recited. It is acted out. Use the available levels, the steps, a chair, a platform.)

Nathan says we should quit talking about it. He says people are getting tired of hearing it and are starting to make fun of us. Besides what good does it do to talk about something you can't prove? I think Nathan is getting old! *I* can prove it happened!

I was there, wasn't I? So was Nathan and Jethro. Old Ephraim says he didn't see or hear anything. The thing is—he slept through it all. Even if he'd been awake he couldn't hear it thunder right in his ear!

First, there was this light. Abner, the rabbi's son says maybe a bunch of the boys played a joke on us and came out there with torches. Abner fancies himself a wit. He's half right. Now, I saw that light. It started as a kind of glow and got brighter and brighter until I could hardly see, it was so bright. Then, in the middle, there was this figure—like a man. Not clear like I see you, but that was the bright light in our eyes. Then he talked, this—whatever he was. That's when he told us about the baby in the manger in Bethlehem. Oh, I know it sounds weird. Believe me, we were scared to death, even though he said not to be afraid. How could we help it? I never heard of anything like that before. I tell you, when he said *go,* I was *ready!* No telling what would happen to us if we didn't.

Then the sound started. The sound? You've surely heard about the *sound*—like a lot of people singing or chanting. Why, sure we could understand the words. "Glory to God in the highest." That's what. Then, "Peace on earth to men of good will." Over and over, until it faded away, like the light.

Talk about *proving* it. Didn't we go to Bethlehem and ask about a newborn baby? Sure enough, there he was, wrapped up good and in the manger in the stable at the inn. Nathan says it was just coincidence. Jethro just keeps his silence now. Nathan's got him thinking people are tired of hearing about it. He says the people have been looking for the Messiah for centuries and wouldn't know how to stop looking. They can stop any time they want to. He's here.

Well, Nathan's older than I am. I guess if we're going to work together I can't argue with him all the time. But I'll keep remembering, over and over. I'm still *young!* I'll keep asking about him. One of these days—you listen to me!—one of these days, everybody's going to *know.* We *did* see the Messiah! We *did.*

15
Christmas Is When—
(A monologue for fun times)

Christmas is when—

—you get a card from Charley and you don't know any Charley.

—you receive a gift from someone who had agreed faithfully that you wouldn't exchange gifts this year. It cost at least $5.00 too.

—the family's old Christmas tree decorations looked faded and droopy when you unpacked them, until your mother priced new ones in the stores.

—you have to share Christmas dinner with your great-aunt Cora who bores everyone with details of her latest ailment. She always has one.

—your married brothers and sisters and their children come to Grandmother's for dinner. The married brothers and sisters dash off immediately afterward to see an old friend, leaving you and Grandmother with the little kids and all the dishes. Grandmother's cross the rest of the day.

Christmas is when—

—you spend more for gifts than you can and face January with no money.

—relatives from out of town bring their dog, who misbehaves on the new rug in your room and you pretend it doesn't matter.

—your brother's wife keeps nagging at your brother to hurry away to visit *her* parents while all the time your mother knows he'd rather stay with her. Things get tense.

—Grandfather balks at dressing up for a kinfolks dinner and wears his oldest slacks with the big darn on the seat and Grandmother is upset. Of course, if one is that old, it hardly matters what he wears.

Christmas is when—

—your mother is accepting compliments on the turkey and your father casually lets out it came from the cafeteria down the street. She's angry and somehow it's all your fault and you have to do the dishes.
—the tree your mother waited thriftily to buy until the last minute suddenly develops "needle dropitis" all over the piled up gifts and begins to look like your father's head—balding.
—your friend forgets and gives you a scarf you gave her last year.
—you get a card from a sensitive friend you forgot, and it is already Christmas Eve.
—there's always the day after when you have to help clear up the mess and the trashmen won't pick up the old Christmas tree and everything looks icky.

Christmas is when—
—your father's gift to your mother is two sizes too small, and he bought it on sale so she can't exchange it. So she gives it to you, and your Dad is mad at you.
—you think if you hear "Silent Night" just one more time blaring in the stores and streets, you'll be ill. Even though you know that a year from now it will have all the charm of the top hit in the ten best recordings.
—the little children enjoy playing with the wrappings more than the gift they enclosed, which cost too much anyway.
—your widowed father brings a lady friend to Christmas dinner and the family watches her as if she were Mata Hari.
—your widowed mother brings a new gentleman friend and the family takes to him as if he were Attila the Hun.

Christmas is when—
—the parts on the little kids' "assemble yourself" toys are missing or don't fit. And you forgot to get batteries anyway.
—you ought to try to forgive and love everybody, even when you know they are really stinkers and all your goodwill won't change them one bit!

Christmas is when—
—once again we remember what Christmas *really* is: it's the beautiful, shining thing that happens in our hearts when

we remember a stable in Bethlehem and a young mother holding a baby close and warm.

16
Christmas Is a Lonely Time

As long as it still was *before* Christmas, I was all right. Even if I couldn't be at home with all the family, I could send gifts to all of them, couldn't I? Shopping in the city is fun. Before Christmas every store bulged with shoppers. Shoppers at Christmas aren't like shoppers any other time. They smile back at me. Even answer my, "Good morning!"

The stores glistened with tinsel and color. Counters overflowed with gifts and wrappings and decorations. Window displays looked bright and happy. The smells from the little bakery on the corner were luscious. Its fruitcakes are famous everywhere, so my landlady says. Although nobody can beat my grandmother at fruitcake!

I can see the family all around the table at home and smell the dinner and taste Gran's fruitcake. But to keep thinking of home only makes the separation worse. Especially in a family as close as ours. I can hear my mother say now, "Why can't you settle down to a job right here in Hartlesville?"

I tried to make her see. "Mom, I need to go on to school."

That hurt her. "My dear, if only I had the money to send you to college."

"Now, Mom, don't worry," I said. "I'll go to school at night and work at something during the day. Don't worry. I'll make it on my own."

She still wanted me to stay. "You're only seventeen. There's a secure job at Frank's. You can work there as long as you like."

I scoffed, "The same old job at the same old money all my life?"

"Security is important, dear," she said.

"Not that important! Mom, I want to be somebody and go somewhere, not just hold down a job."

So here I am, hundreds of miles from Hartlesville, no family, no friends. Oh, I know people, like the grocer and the pharmacist and the people in the office, but friends takes time. They don't happen in three months. I will have friends some day. This I know. But right now—well, before Christmas I shopped and shopped, elbowing my way through the crowds, hunting for just the right gifts. Gifts I could afford. The job doesn't leave much for extravagancies after paying for food, lodging, transportation, and school fees.

The day the package went off to Hartlesville, I wrote a cheerful letter wishing them all a Merry Christmas and telling them how beautiful and exciting the city looked in all its Christmas finery. Two days later my package from home arrived. I put it on my only chair and resisted the temptation to open it then. I waited until last night, Christmas Eve. The gifts so lovingly packed even had a big piece of Gran's fruitcake. That I set aside for today.

Christmas day in the city. Have you ever seen it? You walk down the empty streets which yesterday were filled with people. The dirty snow lingers in the gutters. The occasional pedestrian looks as lonely as you suddenly feel. Those tinsel decorations which gleamed so brightly yesterday are tarnished and tawdry today. Bits of paper clutter the streets, and the whole city looks gray and dirty. The bakery is closed, and the pharmacy. Nothing is open except the fast-food store in the next block. You pass by, and see two people sitting on opposite sides of the dining area. They are the only customers. The only attendant leans vacantly against the counter. Not one is talking to another.

The little park two blocks along is inhabited only by pigeons and the trash dropped yesterday. The windows of the big department store are still decorated, still filled with wares, but they look tired. Then you pass the window which some window dresser planned as a special Christmas touch—the manger scene. You aren't quite eighteen. You stand there alone, looking at the figures: the animals, the Wise Men, the shepherds, Mary, Joseph, and the tiny baby. A family. A wave of homesickness engulfs you.

Has this happened to you? It happened to me. Christmas is miserable and lonely and not one soul in the whole big city cares if I live or die! I look at the little figure of Jesus. Come to think of it, most of the people didn't care if he died either. Why, all his life he must have been homesick! Oh, he had friends. But many of them melted away like that dirty snow when he needed them most.

It's Christmas. It's his birthday! In two months and eleven days I'll have a birthday. I'll be eighteen. By that time, if I try, I can build the beginning of a friendship with someone. Maybe with more than one someone. Being lonely now is only temporary. Maybe Jesus thought of that too.

I took one last look at the manger scene, then walked back to my room. I took off my coat and sat down and ate Grandmother's fruitcake.

17
The Decision

(This monologue is for male or female, twelve to fourteen. It brings up a contemporary problem but does not solve it.)

December eighteenth. One week. Well, not a whole week, if you count off traveling time. Mom and Dad both pressuring me. There ought to be a third choice and then I wouldn't have to decide between them. But my last grandparent died six years ago. For five years I've been deciding who gets me for Christmas, Mom or Dad. As long as I am here with Mom, why not stay? It's easier.

But I haven't seen Dad since August. Dad's a great guy. If I stay here, he won't say anything. But he'll be disappointed. I like his wife. Barbara is nice. She always listens to me as if what I said made sense to her. That's more than it does to me, sometimes.

If I go, then Mom will be alone. At Christmas you ought to have a family around you. My best friend, Bobby, has a big family. Lots of aunts and uncles and one pair of grandparents. They are Italians; and Italians seem to have a lot of fun together. It's so nice and noisy around their house.

Our house is quiet. Until I get a bunch of my friends in. Mom likes that. If I go to Dad for Christmas, it will be quiet here the whole time I'm gone.

If I were twins, we could go both places. Not at the same time. I mean each to one place.

I can still remember before the divorce when we had Christmas all together. Grandmother Hobson was alive then, and we'd go to her house. I can still remember Grandmother and Ellie in the kitchen making pies.

Ellie stayed with Grandmother and took care of her. There'd be a tree with presents and an angel on top. Down the street was a red brick church. They always had a special Christmas program, and we always went. The year I was eight, I said a poem about the shepherds.

We didn't go back to Grandmother's any more because she died the next May. Then came all the trouble and the divorce. Mom and I moved here and Dad stayed in our old town. In our old house. When I go to Dad that's where we live. It looks different because Barbara changed it all around. I hardly remember now how it used to be.

That little town where Grandmother lived is still there, I guess. Probably the red brick church. That's when Christmas seemed so full of love. They say that God is love and Jesus came as a baby because he loved us. I guess so. My Mom says she loves me and my Dad says so, too. In my mind, I guess they do. Just the same, deep down somewhere I don't *really* believe it. It's as if I had been *rejected* for some reason, as if nobody really cared at all. Wonder why that is? No matter what my mind says. It's strange, isn't it?

Now I have to decide. Again. Mom or Dad. Why does there have to be Christmas anyway?

18
"It Came to Pass"

(Choral speaking arrangement for mixed-speaking group with two male and two female soloists.)

ALL: From the family of David will grow a branch.

FEMALES: The Spirit of God is upon him.

MALES: He comes to proclaim the good news to those who are brokenhearted and in deep despair.

FEMALE SOLO 1: O Bethlehem! You are small but you will be the birthplace of our king!

ALL: The birthplace of our king?

FEMALE SOLO 1: In the days of Herod the king of Judea, there was a priest named Zacharias.

ALL: He and his wife Elisabeth were growing old and had no children.

FEMALE SOLO 1: One day the angel Gabriel appeared to Zacharias.

MALE SOLO 1: "You shall have a son and he shall be called John. He will be a great man. He will turn many to the Lord. Above all, he will prepare the way for the coming of the Messiah."

ALL: It came to pass that Elisabeth conceived as the angel said.

FEMALES: Six months later, God sent the same angel Gabriel to Nazareth. He appeared to Elisabeth's young cousin Mary, who was engaged to marry the carpenter, Joseph.

MALE SOLO 1: "Mary, God is good to you. You will bear a son. You will call his name Jesus. He will be the Son of the

Highest."

ALL: Mary was frightened.

FEMALE SOLO 2: "This is impossible! I have no husband!"

MALE SOLO 1: "God's Spirit will come over you and the holy child will be the Son of God. Even now, your cousin Elisabeth, who has been barren, is in her sixth month. With God nothing is impossible."

FEMALE SOLO 2: "So be it as God wills."

FEMALES: Mary went to Elisabeth, and they rejoiced together.

MALES: When Joseph discovered Mary was with child, he first thought of breaking the betrothal.

FEMALES: Quietly, for he was a kind man.

MALES: But in a dream an angel spoke to him.

MALE SOLO 1: "Joseph, don't be afraid to make Mary your wife. The child she carries was conceived by the Holy Spirit."

ALL: So Joseph took Mary for his wife. This was the time Caesar Augustus, the emperor in Rome, decreed that a census should be taken in the Empire. Everyone went to the city of his family to be registered.

MALE SOLO 2: Now Joseph was of the house of David.

MALES: So he went from Nazareth in Galilee to Bethlehem in Judea.

FEMALES: Even though the time for the delivery of the child was near, Mary went with him.

MALE SOLO 2: There was no room for them in the village inn.

FEMALE SOLO 1: So it happened the child was born in a stable.

FEMALES: His bed was a manger.

FEMALE SOLO 1: The same night, out in the hills, shepherds were guarding the sheep. Suddenly a great light surrounded them and an angel appeared.

Females: They cowered in fear!

Male Solo 1: "Don't be frightened! I bring you joyous news. Soon everyone shall know. The Messiah, the Savior, has been born this very night in Bethlehem! You will know it is he when you find a babe wrapped in swaddling clothes, lying in a manger."

All: Suddenly the shepherds heard a great host crying out, "Glory to God in the highest and peace on earth!"

Females: And then the multitude of angels was gone and the shepherds said,

Males: "Quick! Let's go see if what the angel said is true!"

Female Solo 2: They ran to the village and found Mary and Joseph—

Male Solo 2: And the newborn child in the stable.

Female Solo 2: They told the people what they had seen.

Male Solo 2: And everyone was astonished.

All: Mary listened and remembered it all.

Females: Then the shepherds went back to their sheep, thanking God for letting them see the child.

Female Solo 1: For God so loved the world

Male Solo 2: That he gave his only Son to come to earth as a mortal man.

Female Solo 2: So that everyone who believed in him would not die forever,

All: But enjoy eternal life!

19

It's Christmas Again

(For mixed chorus with seven solo speakers, either male or female.)

ALL *(chanting)*: Valentine Day, Fourth of July, Thanksgiving, Christmas. Christmas. Christmas.

SOLO 1 *(dismayed)*: Not Christmas again?

SOLO 2 *(whining)*: So soon?

ALL: Christmas!

SOLO 2: Mother says we've just finished paying *last* year's bills.

ALL: Christmas. Green trees, pink trees, blue trees, white trees, orange trees, what-have-you trees.

SOLO 3: Well, we bought a ni-i-ice artificial tree last year, and it's good for years to come. Half price, too.

ALL: No polluting, no destroying nature! Good!

SOLO 3: It doesn't smell Christmassy, but it won't catch fire either.

ALL: Christmas decorations in the stores everywhere.

SOLO 1: Used to be they decorated the stores right after Thanksgiving. You know when the first decorations go up now? Before Halloween!

ALL: Carols over the loudspeakers all over the store.

SOLO 2 *(desperately)*: If I hear "Silent Night" one more time, I'll scream!

ALL: Ads in the papers, ads in the magazines, ads left at your door. Pages and pages of ads.

FEMALES: Buy this, buy that. Make Christmas *happy*.

MALES: Buy now, pay later. We won't bill you until February.

FEMALES: Make Christmas expensive. Master Charge, Bank Americard, you-name-it-card.

SOLO 4: My little brother wants a dump truck, a set of racing cars, and a bicycle. Imagine that!

SOLO 5: Becky wants a *horse.* Dad says we can't keep a horse in the apartment.

SOLO 6: Frankie wants to go to Colorado for Christmas. For the skiing, you know. It's quite the rage.

SOLO 4: We'll have to go to Grandmother's again for Christmas dinner. It gets so boring!

SOLO 5: My little sister Sue is so young she won't care what she gets. But *Dad's* folks, the grandparents, are sure to give her something expensive. So what can Mom's folks do?

ALL: Buy this, buy that, make Christmas happy! Buy now, pay later. Pay later. Pay later.

SOLO 1: Why did I choose this school? It's a long way from my hometown. I don't know anyone here. I can't afford to go home. All the relatives will be there for Christmas except me! I hate Christmas anyway!

ALL (*sing raggedly*): Santa Claus is coming to town!

SOLO 2: Did you ever believe in Santa Claus? Maybe someone does give you presents you ask for when you are little, and candy, and an orange in your stocking. Maybe for some. In our house we always had a hard time just getting enough to eat. We learned early Santa Claus was just for rich kids.

ALL (*heartily*): Merry Christmas!

SOLO 7 (*sadly, slowly*): I remember Christmas when I was a little kid. . . . A little kid all innocent and clean inside. Why can't I go back and *be* that little kid again. And feel clean once more?

ALL: It doesn't look like Christmas outside. Trees are bare and there's mud everywhere. Things look grubby and dreary.

SOLO 1: What's Christmas anyway? A rip-off, that's what! I'm going to lock my door and sleep through the whole day.

ALL: What is Christmas?

SOLO 5 (*brightly*): Presents!

SOLO 1 (*bored*): Family dinner!

SOLO 2: Bills!

SOLO 3: Trees!

SOLO 4: Carols!

SOLO 6: Decorations!

SOLO 7: Santa Claus?

ALL: WHAT IS Christmas?

SOLOS 1,2: We told you.

ALL: Is that all?

SOLO 2: We-e-ell, I guess that's not all. I guess it's really the birth of a baby.

ALL: Oh-h-h, a birthday party!

SOLO 2: In a way. Because a long time ago, God sent his Son to earth as a human baby.

ALL: Why a baby?

SOLO 6: I don't know. But there he was, a baby. In a stable in Bethlehem. He grew up and died one day on a cross.

ALL: That's sad.

SOLO 6: You better be glad he did! If he hadn't—but he did.

ALL: Then Christmas is a birthday party, really a birthday party?

SOLO 7: For the Son of God.

SOLO 6: All the other things, the trees and presents and getting together—they are fun. But Christmas really is the birthday of the Son of God!

ALL (*awed*): It really is!

20
Santa Comes to Grandmother's House

(This is a dramatic game in which the audience takes part. Divide the audience into the six groups indicated. Rehearse each group in its sound. As the story is read dramatically, each group makes its sound whenever its name is said.
SANTA CLAUS—*Ho, ho, ho!*
GOOD LITTLE BOY—*Aahhhh!*
BAD LITTLE BOY—*Oh-oh!*
GRANDMOTHER'S HOUSE—(sing) *"Be it ever so humble"*
RUDOLPH—*Honk, honk.*
REINDEER—*Clippity clop, clippity clop.*)

One year two little boys went to spend Christmas at GRANDMOTHER'S HOUSE. One was a GOOD LITTLE BOY. The other was a BAD LITTLE BOY.

Now, there was a problem. GRANDMOTHER'S HOUSE didn't have a chimney. How could SANTA CLAUS come down the chimney when GRANDMOTHER'S HOUSE didn't have a chimney? This worried the GOOD LITTLE BOY. But the BAD LITTLE BOY didn't worry. He shouted that SANTA CLAUS had better bring him some presents or he'd punch SANTA CLAUS in the nose! "SANTA CLAUS better find a way in!" he yelled.

So on Christmas Eve they hung their stockings on a chair in the living room of GRANDMOTHER'S HOUSE. And everybody went to bed. GRANDMOTHER'S HOUSE grew quiet.

Meantime, earlier in the evening, away up at the North Pole, SANTA CLAUS hitched up his REINDEER with RUDOLPH in the lead.

SANTA CLAUS said: "RUDOLPH! RUDOLPH are you sure we have everything?"

RUDOLPH and all the REINDEER made a REINDEER noise to show yes. So SANTA CLAUS climbed into his sleigh, and the REINDEER and RUDOLPH pulled SANTA CLAUS up, up into the sky. Across the hills and countryside they went, until they came to GRANDMOTHER'S HOUSE.

"Whoa, there, REINDEER" shouted SANTA CLAUS. "RUDOLPH, who lives here?"

RUDOLPH made another REINDEER noise.

"I see," said SANTA CLAUS. "Who is visiting here at GRANDMOTHER'S HOUSE?"

RUDOLPH made another REINDEER noise.

"Oh," said SANTA CLAUS, "The GOOD LITTLE BOY and the BAD LITTLE BOY. No chimney, I see."

So SANTA CLAUS climbed in the window of GRANDMOTHER'S HOUSE. He said: "That's easier than a chimney anyway! Sometime I must try a door. Now to work."

Now the GOOD LITTLE BOY and the BAD LITTLE BOY were awake. The sound of RUDOLPH and the REINDEER had awakened them. They sneaked downstairs and were hiding behind the sofa. They saw SANTA CLAUS climb in the window.

SANTA CLAUS said, "Here are toys for the GOOD LITTLE BOY. But only sticks and ashes for the BAD LITTLE BOY."

The BAD LITTLE BOY jumped out from behind the sofa. "Oh, no, you don't!" he cried. "Give me some toys, too, or I'll call the police! They'll get you for breaking and entering."

SANTA CLAUS was worried. "I can't be delayed," he said. "The boys and girls are waiting for me and RUDOLPH and my REINDEER. This is blackmail! But, here are your toys, you BAD LITTLE BOY!"

The BAD LITTLE BOY didn't care what SANTA CLAUS called him. The GOOD LITTLE BOY and the BAD LITTLE BOY began to play with their toys. SANTA CLAUS climbed thankfully out the window.

SANTA CLAUS told the whole miserable story to RUDOLPH and the REINDEER. They made a REINDEER noise of sympathy.

"Can they really arrest me?" asked SANTA CLAUS. "What is the world coming to?"

RUDOLPH and the REINDEER made another REINDEER noise of sympathy, as they sped SANTA CLAUS away from GRANDMOTHER'S HOUSE and the GOOD LITTLE BOY and the BAD LITTLE BOY.

The moral is: today the bad guys don't always get what they deserve.

21
Christmas Out of This World
(A dramatic Christmas party)

This party has a central script with the men on Mars and four fun scripts to be done at the points indicated in the script. The skits could be used alone as well.

The stage is divided into two sections: a back section at least four feet deep and the front whatever remains of the space. A scrim is the divider. A real scrim is a coarsely woven net curtain. When the space in front is lighted and the back part dark, actors behind the scrim are not seen. Conversely, if the back part is lighted and no lights are in front, the area is highly visible. A real scrim is expensive. Unless you plan to use it often, a substitute is the best choice. Here is a relatively inexpensive substitute. From a wallpaper store buy an ample supply of the cheapest wall canvas. This will be something like cheesecloth, but firmer. Stretch a wire across the stage. Trim away the selvage edges of the canvas and drape across the wire so that both ends touch the floor. Overlap these strips, "fulling" them on generously. The audience will see a graceful curtain when the lights are on in front of it.

Behind the scrim at one side is a portion of a spaceship. The wall behind has planets and stars. Two *Martians* are the actors behind the scrim. They wear allover suits of green. Make the bodies bulbous with padding, the legs thin, and the feet extra large. The head is covered with a green hood, face and all. It has two pointed noses, one huge eye, one round mouth, no ears, and a green antennae on top (pipe cleaners). The hands have three fingers.

The forestage has a Christmas tree at one side.

You may add other skits to those printed here. The more people involved, the more successful will be your party.

Begin the party with something for the early birds to do, such as making Christmas cards. Start activities with group singing of carols and popular Christmas songs. The master of ceremonies introduces Professor Umtwaddle who has invented a miraculous cosmic paint. It will enable us to see life on Mars. The professor brings in a paint bucket and brush and paints the air in front of the audience.

Auditorium lights off. Mars lights on.

Scene: One *Martian* standing right; other climbs from spaceship. They greet each other Martian style, using gestures freely to make meanings clear throughout.

HUROK: Eeefoo, Golo!

GOLO: Eeefoo, Hurok! You space tripped?

HUROK (*nodding*): Lup, Golo, lup! Mine viewed Moon and Earth.

GOLO: Moon unfurnished, mine cognize. Mine not viewed earth. Unfurnished?

HUROK: Nob. Furnished. Leems (*gestures "trees" and "plants"*), iggles (*gesture "birds"*), opps (*points to self*) designate "people"!

GOLO: Opps—"people?" (*He giggles at the unfamiliar word.*) Aspect? (*Show he is asking if people look like Martians.*)

HUROK (*shakes head*): Nob! (*When he calls out these features have him hold up fingers to show earth people have two eyes, one nose, one mouth, as he points to his own weird features.*) Loo! (*nose*) Ock! (*eyes*) Ippu! (*mouth*). (*Points to side of the head where Martians have no ears*) "Ears."

GOLO (*amazed*): "Ears?" Nob ips? (*Points to antennae.*)

HUROK: Nob! (*They laugh heartily.*)

GOLO: Mine yearn view people. Doing?

HUROK: Christmas. You yearn view "Christmas?"

GOLO (*sighing*): Lup, lup!

HUROK (*reaches in spaceship and picks up a box. Points it toward the audience as Golo watches*): View Christmas! View people! Christmas bygone.

Lights off Mars. Lights on Front.

Skit: "The Gift Went Round and Round."

Lights off Front. Lights on Mars. (Get props on stage for pantomime: chair, pallet bed, big box with girl in it.)

GOLO (*puzzled*): Christmas? Christmas wokky!

HUROK (*indicating yes and no*): Wokky! Lup and nob.

GOLO (*rejecting*): Christmas wokky! (*Starts off.*)

HUROK (*firmly*): View Christmas more!

GOLO: M-m-m Lup.

Lights off Mars. Lights on Front.

Pantomime. Either the one following this script or one of your own. Classical music is excellent for pantomimes.

Lights off Front. Lights on Mars.

GOLO (*still puzzled*): Christmas? People nubok! (*Show he means crazy.*)

HUROK (*holding out box*): Lup! View Christmas, Golo.

Lights off Mars. Lights on Front.

Skit: "A Christmas Triangle"

Lights off Front. Lights on Mars. (Props for next skit placed at sides of stage: small settee, occasional tables, other chairs.)

GOLO (*showing pleasure*): Christmas!

HUROK: Lup, lup.

GOLO (*puzzled, points to his finger remembering the ring*): Hurok?

HUROK (*holding up one finger*): Pika.

GOLO: Pika?

HUROK: Pika! (*He goes through elaborate motions of putting a ring on Golo's finger. Golo dissolves into giggles because it tickles.*)

HUROK (*sternly*): *Pika!* (*Once more he goes through motions of putting the ring on Golo's finger.*) Pika!

GOLO (*dreamily*): Pika. (*He looks admiringly at his finger.*)

HUROK: View Christmas!

Lights off Mars. Lights on Front.

Skit: The Unwanted Guest" (*As family comes on stage they pull the furniture into place and then sit to plan.*)

Lights off Front. (*In the dark pull the furniture off fast. Set up manger scene.*)

Lights on Mars.

GOLO (*still puzzled at people*): Christmas! Nob mine want.

HUROK: Christmas another.

GOLO: Christmas another?

HUROK: Lup. View Christmas!

Lights off Mars. (*In dark, let manger scene tableau take place.*)

Lights on Front.

Tableau: the manger scene while someone reads Luke 2:1-12. Then without accompaniment let everyone sing "Silent Night."

Auditorium lights up as master of ceremony thanks the professor for the view of Christmas out of this world. Refreshment time.

22

The Gift Goes Round and Round

(*It is after Christmas.* Sue *and* Greta *are walking down the street and meet* Martha.)

MARTHA: Sue! Greta! How nice to see you. Did you have a good Christmas?

SUE: Lovely! You never saw so many gifts.

GRETA: Me, too. Didn't you go to your grandmother's for

Christmas, Martha?

MARTHA: Yes, and we had snow and more fun. All the aunts and cousins and relatives came and we had one of those big dinners where you eat and eat and eat. I know I gained five pounds!

SUE: Thank you for the darling jewel box. You have no idea how it brought order out of chaos.

MARTHA: I'm so glad you liked it, Sue. Thank you for the perfume. My favorite. Such a big bottle.

SUE: I knew you like that scent. What did Greta give you, Martha?

GRETA: I knew you were giving her perfume, so I gave her a jeweled atomizer.

MARTHA: It's just beautiful.

SUE: What did Martha give you, Greta?

GRETA: Well—now that you ask—that *is* peculiar. It has me puzzled. She gave me a—well, a large Grecian urn!

SUE (*horrified*): Oh, no!

GRETA: Oh *yes!* A large Grecian urn about four feet tall. Sue. A peculiar shade of green with Grecian gods and goddesses embossed all over it. And standing on an ebony pedestal!

MARTHA (*to Sue, defensively*): Sue, I'm sorry you found out. I simply couldn't think of a thing to get Greta and I know she goes in for stuff like that and I know you gave me that urn last Christmas, but I couldn't use it and I know I said I loved it and it was just what I wanted and I know you won't forgive me but it's too late now and—(*She realizes that Sue and Greta have been looking at each other and growing more and more amused.*)—and—what's the matter? Aren't you mad at me, Sue?

SUE and GRETA (*laughing together hilariously*): No! Oh, no!

MARTHA (*rather put out*): I don't see what's so funny.

SUE (*laughing*): Oh, Martha! Oh, it's too funny!

GRETA (*laughing*): I can't believe it! (*Laughing harder.*)

MARTHA (*a little miffed*): I must say this is a strange way to take it. After all I did give Greta the present you gave me last Christmas, but not very many people would think it was funny! They'd be mad!

GRETA: *I* couldn't be mad! Oh, Martha! You don't know how funny—

SUE (*still laughing*): And *I* couldn't be mad, because—(*laughing again*)—because—*Greta* gave *me* that urn Christmas before last!

(*All keep on laughing hilariously as they walk off.*)

23

A Christmas Pantomime

Classical music is excellent for pantomimes, which are dramas without words. This one is planned for Rossini's "Italians in Algeria Overture." You may wish to use something else and work out your own pantomime. This one uses a straight chair, a pallet bed, and a big box large enough to hold a real girl. The box has Christmas paper pasted on and a lid which lifts off. There is a big bow pasted on top. The girl in the box is dressed as a baby doll. Two girls in children's gowns or pajamas and a mother and father make up the rest of the cast. As the music begins, the doll is in the box. The parents enter with the two girls and tuck them in.

The girls pretend to go to sleep. The mother looks at the Christmas tree and pats the bow on the box. The parents tiptoe over and look at the children (*this is the soft intro*). At the sudden heavy chord, the father sneezes and mother shushes him and they tiptoe out (*as the quiet music ends*).

(*Music increases in volume and tempo.*) Girls were awake all the time. They get up and go to door to listen for parents. (*Music picks up.*) They run around the tree happily. They see the box. (*During a definite pause in the music*) They are tempted to open the box, arguing with each other and finally deciding to do it. They lift the lid and see the doll (*as the music crescendos*). They lift the doll out. (*There is plenty of time to get her out as the crescendo ends.*)

They sit her on the floor and admire her. The doll is completely limp and sits however they place her, falling if she isn't balanced right. (*The more limp she is, and the more she falls, the funnier it is.*) They admire her dress and hair. When the happy little flute part begins, they dance around her. During a heavier passage they run to the door and listen and return to play with the doll.

As the music crescendos, they drag the doll to a chair and try to sit it in the chair. It keeps sliding off, and they keep trying to make it stay (*all during the loud movement*). Then (*at a sudden softness*) they think they hear their parents. They frantically try to put the doll back in the box. Arms and legs keep flopping out with the emphatic blasts of sound. As the quick loud section comes to a close, they get her in and the box closed and jump into bed.

When the flute parts begin again the parents enter to check and are happy at the peace and quiet. They look at the tree and the box and leave again. As the crescendo begins, the girls quickly unpack the doll and lift her to their bed, fixing the top back on the box. They jump into bed and cover themselves and the doll as the music ends.

24

A Christmas Triangle

Props: mistletoe and decorations

Cast: Beth, who has just broken with Bill; Francie, her best friend; Bill.

(*The girls enter to finish decorating. Beth is dejected and Francie tries to cheer her up. They bring decorations.*)

Francie: It won't take long to finish decorating in here. You'll feel better if you are busy. (*They take opposite sides of the stage to work.*)

BETH (*mournfully*): Well, it has just ruined Christmas for me. Why, Bill and I have been going steady for two whole years. Almost. Now this. How about putting this stuff here?

FRANCIE: Oh, anywhere. Beth, that's no way for you to feel. I know lots of boys who would like to date you, but Bill's always around.

BETH: You never did like for me to go with Bill, did you?

FRANCIE (*quickly*): It wasn't that, Beth! I just never felt he was good enough for you is all.

BETH (*resolutely*): Well, I'll just have to get over him, because this time it's final, I'm afraid.

FRANCIE: Maybe you really have been ready to break with him for a long time, but he has been such an old habit with you that you didn't know it. I'd better fasten this green stuff up.

BETH: That's mistletoe. Maybe you're right. There are a lot more boys around! Bill isn't the only one—even if he does think so!

FRANCIE (*looking at her thoughtfully*): Now that you've brought it up, he *is* conceited I think, and has an inflated opinion of how wonderful he is! To hear him tell it, his taste is perfect and his opinions are always right! You know, Beth, I never did think he was right for you. You've done a smart thing.

BETH: Perhaps. But it is all over now. When we meet, I'll treat him just like anybody else—a friend. An old friend!

FRANCIE: I think you are being very sensible about this. Now if you will just hold fast to your resolution—even when you see Bill with another girl.

BETH (*sharply*): Another girl! . . . Well . . . I . . . of course I'll stick to it! What do I care how many girls he has? He's a free agent, isn't he?

FRANCIE: I'm glad you feel that way. I'm your best friend, and I'm glad you're so sensible.

(Bill enters, unexpectedly. Beth assumes an indifferent attitude. Francie looks at Beth apprehensively, sees how she is taking it, then goes all out in greeting Bill.)

FRANCIE (*squealing*): *Bill!* How *wonderful!* You can help us decorate for the party.

BILL: Hi, Francie. Uh—hello, Beth.

BETH (*doesn't look up from her work*): Hello, Bill.

BILL: Uh—how have you been?

BETH (*coldly*): Quite well, thank you. And you?

BILL (*shifting uncomfortably*): Oh! Uh—okay, I guess.

FRANCIE (*quickly*): See what you think of this, Bill. Is it fastened tight enough to stay until the party is over? (*He comes and tests it.*) I always did think you had such excellent judgment! (*Beth looks at her in amazement. Francie sees this and continues in a low tone to Bill. Apparently Beth can't hear her now.*) Bill, you have my sympathy. Beth has no right to treat you like this! Not that it isn't a good thing, even if I *am* her best friend. The truth is, Bill, that Beth just doesn't appreciate you at all!

BILL (*visibly brightening under her flattery*): You think so?

FRANCIE: Of course I do! Now, if you'd been my steady I'd have known how to treat you.

BILL (*more cheerful*): You would, Francie?

FRANCIE: I would! My gracious, where does Beth think she'll ever find another boy with your talent and looks and taste and intellect? (*She draws near and touches his arm caressingly.*)

BILL (*happily*): Oh, now, Francie, you are just saying that to make me feel good.

FRANCIE: Bi-i-ill! How can you say that! It is just the truth.

BILL: Now, Francie, I didn't mean it that way. Here, let me help you. (*He picks up a piece of mistletoe.*) Where were you going to put this?

FRANCIE: I thought it would add greenery to the wall here.

BILL (*playfully*): A wall is no place for mistletoe! Who can stand under a wall? (*Looks at ceiling*) It ought to hang down from there. (*He holds the mistletoe high and over Francie, who is enjoying this.*) Now, it should be about this high—and like this—to give an excuse for this! (*He leans forward and kisses Francie quickly. She pretends surprise even though she saw it coming. Beth is watching the entire by-play jealously.*)

FRANCIE (*pretending confusion*): Oh, Bill! You shouldn't!

BILL (*with satisfaction*): Why not? That's what it's for, isn't it? Such a little piece of green with such possibilities!

(*Beth crosses the stage and jerks the mistletoe from Bill.*)

BETH: I need this piece please! (*She marches angrily back. Bill follows while Francie watches and then slowly resumes her work.*)

BILL: That was a little uncalled for, wasn't it?

BETH: I don't know what you mean, I'm sure!

BILL: Oh, yes you do. Would you be jealous by any chance?

BETH (*laughing falsely*): Me? Jealous? How ridiculous. It doesn't make any difference to me how disgracefully you act in public! You are no concern of mine, Bill Wentworth!

BILL: For someone so indifferent, you are certainly making a mountain out of a molehill!

BETH: Molehill! You call it a molehill when my best friend—my *best friend*—and a boy I've given the best years of my life—when they act so disgustingly right before my eyes?

BILL (*drawing closer*): They were good years, weren't they, Beth?

BETH (*tearfully*): Yes, they were! And you're trying to spoil a beautiful memory!

BILL (*removes decorations from Beth's hands and gives her his handkerchief*): They don't have to be just a memory. It was your idea you know. You said we'd gone together too long.

BETH (*blowing her nose loudly*): It was too long! (*She begins crying again.*) Here it is another Christmas and you'd give me something that didn't matter when what I really wanted was your class ring! (*Wailing now.*) And you didn't do anything and I'm tired and mis-s-serable! Oh, Bill! (*She is crying on his shirtfront, and he is patting her back consolingly.*)

BILL: Now, there's nothing to cry about. I came over here to make up with you, not to fight some more.

BETH: Oh, Bill!

BILL: Look, here's the ring! (*He takes it from his finger and places it on hers. They walk off slowly, his arm around her. She keeps on talking, looking admiringly at the ring.*)

BETH: Oh, Bill! I'm so happy! It's the most beautiful Christmas gift I ever saw! Oh, Bill!

(*Francie watches them leave, then looks at the audience and shrugs. She picks up the box of decorations and leaves.*)

25
Unwanted Guest

This skit is one in which the actors work out their own lines following the plot. In rehearsal, the right lines will stay and the unneeded will be dropped.

Setting: the Hunter home

Cast: the family: Vera, the mother; Philip, the father; Eileen, the daughter; Rick, the son; and Great-aunt Veronica.

The young friends who help out: painter, musician, building repairmen, wrestlers or judo experts, "crazy woman and keepers," "hoods," repossessors.

Situation: Family has planned a pleasant Christmas with their friends. They receive word that Great-aunt Veronica is coming to spend the holidays. They are upset because she is an opinionated, domineering old lady who dislikes social occasions and makes life unpleasant for the family while she is there. Let the dialog show this as the family gathers for a council of war. The two teenagers resolve to make things so unpleasant for Great-aunt Veronica that she will go home.

Development: The old lady arrives and is as unpleasant as possible. She takes over the living room and dictates the kind of Christmas she wants: no noise, no company, and no young people around because her nerves are edgy. She wants just a quiet Christmas at home with the family.

The teenagers go off to plan with their friends on how to oust her. Left with the parents, the old lady criticizes their home, their appearance, and their habits. When they have all they can take, they leave her, ostensibly to do some shopping.

The two teenagers return. Then the parade of their friends begins. They pretend to be as bewildered as the aunt by the ensuing confusion.

First: An artist with easel and a musician with guitar appear. Artist sets up her easel, moving and disturbing the aunt in the process. Musician, using full volume, practices chords, hitting wrong ones.

Then: A couple of building repairmen come to check on a leaky ceiling. They set up ladders, again moving furniture and aunt, and talk about planned work. The aunt is more upset by the confusion. She loses her temper, and there is a five-way argument all at once. The musician, the artist, and the repairmen take their tools and leave.

Next: A "crazy" woman enters with two "keepers." She says that this is the railroad station and she is waiting for a train. She decides Aunt Veronica is a thief who will steal her purse, and the keepers beg everyone to humor her lest she become violent. She makes the keepers search Aunt Veronica before she leaves. The old lady is frightened and humiliated but still master of their fates!

Then: Two "hoods" run in, fleeing the law. They argue whether to kill Aunt Veronica when she tries to intimidate them or to lock her in a closet so she can't call the police. Her nerves are going by the time they do.

Next: Two wrestlers or judo experts enter with mat. They move furniture to the sides of the room and also Aunt Veronica when she tries to interfere. They tell her they have rented the living room for a practice hall. They create confusion practicing and then propose to practice on Aunt Veronica, choosing her over the teenagers because she has been so interfering. The teenagers persuade them to leave without harming the old lady.

So: She collapses in a chair just as movers come to repossess the furniture for nonpayment. They push her around as they take it all, even when she offers to pay. "The front office will have to take care of that. We're just paid to get the stuff."

Finally: The parents return and are bewildered at what has happened. Great-aunt Veronica cannot be persuaded to stay but decides to go visit another relative for Christmas. They bid her farewell. When she has gone, the whole cast returns to rejoice that they can go ahead with their party plans.